STRUCK LIGHTNING

THEN BY LOVE

Wilma Stanchfield
with Helen Kooiman Hosier

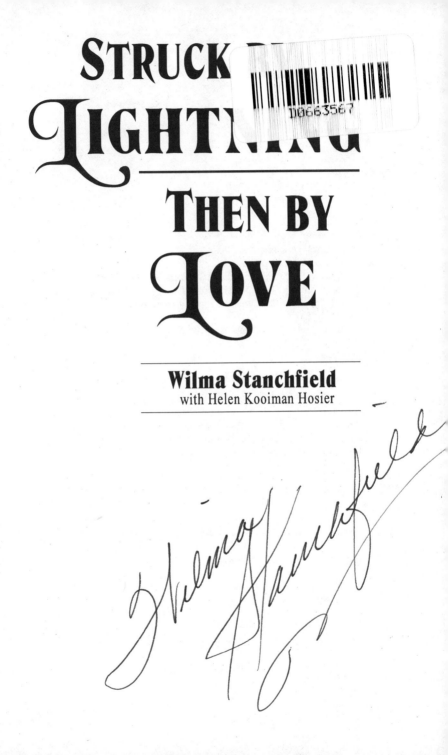

Printed in the United States of America.

Library of Congress Cataloging in Publication Data

Stanchfield, Wilma.
 Struck by lightning, then by love.

 1. Stanchfield, Wilma. 2. Converts—United States—
Biography. I. Hosier, Helen Kooiman, joint author.
II. Title.
BV4935.S66A37   248′.24 [B]   79-13763
ISBN 0-8407-5690-9

Dedication

This book was written in memory of my wonderful, loving dad, Leslie Burrows, who preferred to be known as "Jim", and my brother Jim. I know my father's faithful prayers for my brother and me for over thirty years were responsible for our receiving Jesus Christ as our Lord and Savior.

A homebuilder by trade, Dad found himself in dire financial situations at times during the Depression. It was often necessary for him to take risky jobs in his effort to keep his little family together. I vividly remember his taking a job on the Columbia River as a logger, an extremely hazardous occupation at best. For Dad it was extra dangerous, because he couldn't swim.

Dad, who was both father and mother to us for many years, became a Christian when I was a young girl. I wasn't aware of it then, but I now know that from that time on, Dad spent considerable time on his knees asking our Lord to bring my younger brother and me into God's kingdom.

As the years passed, Dad worked his way up the economic ladder until he was foreman in a large paper mill. He held this position for many years, until he developed emphysema and had to take early retirement. All through these years, until his death, he steadfastly continued to pray for his two children.

With God, all things are possible; in His perfect time, He honored my father's prayers. He arranged circumstances so that both my brother and I became Christians, first me and then my brother.

My brother, a college professor for years, received his doctorate in law in 1968; national recognition with an award as outstanding educator of America in 1970; Jesus Christ as his Lord and Savior in 1973; and his greatest award, being called home to be with Jesus, in 1976.

I want to pay tribute to my father's loving prayers and to our God, who answers prayers. How good it is to *know* where Dad and Jimmie are. What a blessing to know I will see them again when we are all gathered together with Jesus.

Acknowledgments

What joy it gives me to acknowledge and thank the Lord for bringing the Darrell Lundgrens to live next door to us as loving neighbors. Their kind acts and gentle persistence finally brought me to where I invited Jesus into my life.

My thanks for the marvelous and unique organization, the Christian Women's Club. The instrument that God uses so *effectively* in the lives of women like me brings us to know the reality of God's love through Jesus Christ.

I thank Ellen Thiessen for the deep insight and understanding she showed as she led the first Bible study I seriously attended during my early growth as a Christian.

With loving appreciation I acknowledge my pastor, Ken Churchill, and his lovely wife, Marie, for their patience and untiring love in teaching me and our family the Word of God every Friday evening for many years at Bible studies in our home.

I also thank my college professors at Northwestern College night school, and other teachers who helped me better understand God's Word.

My sincere thanks to the many authors and publishers of numerous Christian books that have influenced my thinking. As new ideas of God's truth become at home in my thoughts, it is almost impossible for me to tell whether these insights come directly from God, my own imagination, or from the many contributions of these numerous authors whose works I have read. If I should inadvertently use some of their expressions, I know they will thank the Lord that their ministry is being carried forward by this new branch of the vine.

I give my loving and deepest gratitude to my wonderful husband, Roald, my precious daughter, Marlisa, and all the other supportive family members who steadfastly stood by me during many of the fiery trials of my Christian growth.

I acknowledge the love of God that gave me my dear, close friend and prayer partner, Elaine Gabriel. She is *always* there with a helping hand, undertaking many tasks to help my growing ministry. She is the most *giving* person I've ever met! Elaine is truly God's appointed helper to me, and I am exceedingly grateful.

Finally, I praise God for His perfect timing for this book as He led me to meet Helen Kooiman Hosier. I had admired, enjoyed, and shared her book *Cameos—Women Fashioned by God* many times; and I feel strongly that God arranged our coming together for His glory in this venture of writing my first book.

Foreword

It took a thunderous bolt of lightning for God to gain our attention and to persuade my wife and me to search for truth and reality and to ask that all-important question "Where am I going to spend eternity?"

Statistics reveal that the chances of anyone being struck by lightning are one in a million. The chances of being struck by lightning and living to tell about it are even more remote. The chances of anyone over forty years old becoming a Christian are also slim.

In contrast to these long odds, what do you think the chances are for someone over forty to become a Christian after he or she has been struck by lightning? If he or she miraculously retains full mental faculties, the odds become perhaps fifty-fifty.

As this book reveals in exciting detail, this was our situation. In answer to the earnest prayers of Jim, my wife's father, God arranged the circumstances. They may seem a little extreme, as is sometimes necessary with hard heads like us; but

His measures were effective. He had our undivided attention!

Naturally we do not recommend that anyone wait for such violent action before they look to God. It could be fatal! It is our sincere hope that this book will come into the hands of people who, not knowing Jesus Christ, will realize what a precarious situation they are in, and act now.

Our fortunes can change drastically in an instant. We use the expression "Fast as a flash of lightning." That is exactly how our lives changed. One moment we were in perfectly good health; the next we were dying from a flash of lightning. Wilma describes how it is possible to die without knowing God—and how awful it is at that time to be totally aware of the presence of Almighty God but to be falling away from Him—all because you have never stopped long enough to know Him! There can be no greater tragedy than this.

You or I can be enjoying a drive in our automobile one moment, and involved in a serious accident the next. We can be in perfect health one second, and deathly sick the next. We can be here on Earth one moment, and in heaven or hell the next. Which will it be? That is the all-important question. Where will we spend eternity?

The experiences referred to in this book are *true*. They really happened. Wilma and I *know* there is life after death.

Roald A. Stanchfield

CHAPTER 1

My Introduction
to Wilderness Camping

Never underestimate the power of prayer or the significance of a praying parent. I was raised in a one-parent home by a hard-working father who, when he wasn't working on the treacherous Columbia River as a logger to support his two children, spent much of his time praying for those children, whose mother had walked out on them.

I never forgot the trauma of Mother's leaving us. It is a vivid and painful memory. "I am going out," she said as she walked out the door.

I wanted to say, "But where are you going, Mama?" But all I could do was lift my arms to try to hug and kiss her. She responded by pushing me away. "No, no, you will mess my face."

I experienced rejection that was to shape the next years of my life in a destructive way.

By the time I was twenty-five I had one defunct marriage and an alienated mother behind me. When Roald (pronounced "rolled") Stanchfield walked into my life in 1949, I met a very distinguished, handsome man. He is Norwegian and Welsh, with a quiet spirit and a gentleness that drew me to him. He was very kind, open, generous, and loving. These were all the things I needed and hungered for. Our love for each other went through four years of testing before we finally married. I immediately inherited a family of three children.

Two years after I married Roald, the twins—at that time sixteen—remarked to their father that it would be nice if Wilma knew more about the marvelous sport that everyone enjoys in Minnesota: wilderness camping. I was from the West Coast and unfamiliar with this type of sport. Not knowing better, I said, "Let's go!" This was my first mistake.

Mistake number two was when they said, "May we take a couple of friends along?" and I said, "The more the merrier!" Thus I found myself, one hot, August morning, with four sixteen-year-old boys, a husband, a canoe tied on top of a station wagon, and two weeks of supplies, heading for northern Minnesota to a town called International Falls on the shores of Rainy Lake.

Shortly after arriving we rented a boat and made arrangements to leave our station wagon for two weeks. We tied the canoe on the boat, loaded kids and supplies, and were off. We struck off across the lake to find an island where I could enjoy wilderness camping. Rainy Lake is beautiful and very big. Forty miles out, almost to the Canadian border, we finally landed on what was to be our home for the next two weeks.

My Introduction to Wilderness Camping

As we set up camp, I found out why everybody had been so gung-ho on my coming along. They needed a cook. We got there on Thursday, and by Saturday I was thoroughly disenchanted with this thing they called "sport." I was having no fun—I was washing dishes, cooking, washing dishes. It was a constant round, and those four boys did eat!

I was beginning to think I must have been crazy. More than once I asked myself, *How did you get yourself into this?* Because I was their stepmother, I did not want the boys to know that I could get very disgruntled about situations like this, and I surely didn't want their friends to know. I did what I was long accustomed to doing when I found myself in circumstances that weren't particularly to my liking—I whipped out the kind of mask I needed to put on an act and tried to think my way out of the situation which I had unwittingly gotten into. I thought, *If this is their idea of a vacation for dear ole Mom, they can keep it. This is terrible, the food won't last two weeks, and, in any event, I'm sure I won't last as long as the food!*

Saturday night I crawled into my sleeping bag, exhausted but thinking hard: *How can I get myself out of this?* I came to what I thought was a good solution. I fell into a sound sleep, assuring myself that by the following day I'd have the situation well in hand. The next morning I crawled out of the sleeping bag, ready to put my plan into action. But I heard a strange sound and looked out of the tent.

Plop, plop, plop, at first, and then so many *plop-plops* I knew unmistakably that what I was hearing was water striking canvas. Have you ever been wilderness camping in the rain? I looked back into the tent at my husband, still snug in his sleeping bag. At that point I made a very profound statement. "We might have known we'd get rain. After all, this isn't called Rainy Lake for nothing!"

Poking my head out the tent flap, I observed the gray, bleak morning. *Well, what do I do now?* I already knew the answer. *Make breakfast, Wilma, that's the plan.*

I had wanted to shake my husband, run to the other tent and shake the boys, and grandly announce, "You know, I have not been fair to you. I have been just hogging all the joys of this wilderness camping—cooking and washing dishes, and cooking some more—and it's just not nice of me. I apologize, and I am going to correct this by sharing the joys with you. . . ."

Obviously, this wasn't the morning to put the plan into action.

I began to fix breakfast gloomily—my mood matched the inclemency of the day. The aroma of bacon frying and coffee boiling brought the camp to life. Soon I was joined by my husband and the four boys. They all ate heartily, as usual—I could not believe the quantities of food these men were able to consume—and I continued frying more bacon, fixing more flapjacks and eggs, and refilling cups with coffee. I washed the dishes, my mood changing from gloomy gray to dismal black. The wind blew harder, and it grew darker outside. Claps of thunder and flashes of lightning made me suspect we were in for an electrical storm.

I now know that safety rules say if you are caught outdoors during an electrical storm, you should lie down and stay on low ground. The worst thing you can do is to seek shelter under a lone tree, or stand atop a hill or near a lake.

Not only were we under trees, but we were, of course, near the lake. We watched from the shelter of the tent as the wind skipped across the lake, forming whitecaps. We noticed a little activity on the lake. We were really in the wilderness and had not seen so much as an animal since our arrival. But this was Sunday morning, and a few boats were out on the lake with fishermen trying their luck.

As I stood watching, I noted one boat coming into our particular point. The boat came in with a flourish and four people jumped out—two couples in what I guessed to be their mid-sixties. They rapidly secured the boat and came running up. "We're going to have a storm; may we take shelter here with you?"

Roald said, "Glad to have you. Wilma, get the coffee."

Then Roald tried to soothe our guests: "We're not going to have much of a storm. It's really nothing to worry about. It will blow over soon." But there were sound effects from the department upstairs, voicing a different opinion! Suddenly the sky was lit up by a brilliant flash of lightning, and there was a resounding crash of thunder. I leaped into the air and noted, as I was coming down, that another boat was pulling in. I looked at the people jumping out, securing their boat, and said, "We *are* going to have a storm. Look, they're coming in too."

"No, no, Wilma, there's no problem; they are just getting off the water because of a little electrical activity," Roald insisted. Again there were more sound effects to the contrary. This time Roald leaped into the air. "Well, we'll just have to wait this thing out," he remarked. "It won't be long and it will be over."

I had moved to another part of the tent, when Roald said, "Wilma, look." We stood in the flapway of the tent with our arms around each other, just peering out at one of the most spectacular sights I had ever seen. Rainy Lake is noted for the beauty of its storms. It was a sight of awesome beauty as the cloud formations moved with the dazzling forked lightning flashing through the sky. It was the flashiest phenomenon either of us had ever seen.

In recent years I have learned that lightning kills more people (on the average) per year than hurricanes and tornadoes combined. Lightning blasts through the atmosphere at an estimated rate of 2 billion flashes a year. In the United States alone, it kills one person and injures four others every day.[1] Yet, the chances of being struck by lightning are about one in a million. The chances of being struck and surviving are even more remote.

Scientists have found that one stroke of lightning produces more than 15 million volts. A spark between a cloud and the Earth may measure as much as eight miles long, traveling at a rate of 100 million feet a second. Lightning reaching between oppositely charged clouds may have a length of twenty miles.

Lightning between clouds doesn't cause damage on Earth, since the electrical energy is dispersed in the air. But lightning between a cloud and the Earth often causes loss of life and property. If a man could find a way to use the electrical current in a single lightning flash a mile long, he could light a million lightbulbs.

Lightning travels at an incredible speed. These bolts heat up and burn the air while passing through it. This is what causes the flash. The roar of thunder which follows is caused by the vacuum created by the lightning as air molecules collide or explode in their rush to fill the vacated area.

As Roald and I stood together in the door of the tent, arms wrapped around each other, we didn't know all these things about lightning. But we did know we were witnessing one of nature's strangest phenomena. We continued watching as the waves rolled up and the sky was lit up like

[1]*The World Book Encyclopedia*, Vol. 12 (Chicago: Field Enterprises Educational Corporation, 1973).

brilliant fireworks. "Isn't that beautiful?" Roald observed. "I'm going to try to take a picture of it."

My husband leaned over to get his camera, which was in the corner of the tent, and at that moment, the last thing in the world that can happen, did happen. It always happens to someone else, but this time it happened to us. My husband and I were struck by lightning.

CHAPTER 2

Struck by Lightning

Do you have any idea what it feels like to die when you do not know God? You know the Bible stories perhaps, and some of the words recorded in the Bible, but you do not know Him. In the moment I was hit, I knew exactly what had happened to me. I did not lose consciousness; my mind was crystal clear. When you are struck you neither see nor hear a thing, and yet, in the moment I was dying, I had never been so totally alive.

I was completely paralyzed. I plummeted headlong into what is best described as a pit. I was alone. I had no idea Roald had been struck. He had no idea I had been struck. As I fell, thoughts began to go clearly through my mind.

My first thought: *I wonder if Roald knows that I am dying.* Then, very clearly, the next thought: *It doesn't matter, Wilma. It is beside the point. The point is that you are dying, and you did not think it could happen to you.* Another thought followed: *It's also beside the point that just a few moments ago you were very disgruntled about wilderness*

camping, *but it really doesn't matter anymore.*
Still another thought: *Also beside the point are all
those plans you had for your life.*

Oh, I had all kinds of things I was going to do,
and expectations for our marriage. I was still
young, but now it was all beside the point. Time
had run out.

Still clearly, thoughts began to pass through my
mind of all the things I had done in my life—
hidden, secret things that I had been sweeping
under the carpet of life, so to speak, for years.
Whenever I happened to recall something from
the past that I wished had not happened, I always
felt that someday I must find out what one does
with things of this sort. How do you handle the
regrettable things of the past? But I had never
taken the time to find out. Now I was thinking: *It's
all beside the point. Time is running out.*

At this point in the act of dying, I had what I call
the answer to a question I had never verbalized to
anyone or even faced myself. I cannot communicate this in the way it actually happened. It is
quite indescribable, but at that moment the total-
ity and reality of the living God exploded within
my being, and I knew He was real. It was an
awareness. A total awareness. God filled every
atom of my body. *Every pore of my being was
aware of the glory of the living God.*

Then, to my horror, I found I was falling away
from this glorious God instead of toward Him. It
was as though I was given one moment to know

completely what could have been, only to go another way. In my panic, I reached into this vast storehouse we call the mind, and began to rummage for something to sustain me, something to communicate to the God I knew was there. I pulled out, of all things, the Twenty-third Psalm. I do not remember having learned this. Perhaps a Sunday school teacher taught it to me as a child—I don't know. However, it sprang full-blown into my mind, and I began to pray it to the God I knew was there.

The LORD is my shepherd; I shall not want. He maketh me to lie down in green pastures: he leadeth me beside the still waters. He restoreth my soul: he leadeth me in the paths of righteousness for his name's sake. . . (Ps. 23:1–3).

Years later I was to discover Hebrews 4:12 in the Bible.

For the word of God is quick, and powerful, and sharper than any twoedged sword, piercing even to the dividing asunder of soul and spirit, and to the joints and marrow, *and is a discerner of the thoughts and intents of the heart* (italics added).

That is true. As I said the words of the Twenty-third Psalm to God while dying, they seemed to cut through to where I really lived. I found myself saying, "But You aren't my Shepherd, are You? I want to live. God, if You let me live, I will do anything for You. I'll pay You back. I'll give my life to You. Anything, anything God. Let me live!"

At the same time Roald had plummeted headlong into his pit, and he, too, was alone. At the time of being struck, he was reaching down with his left hand to pick up the camera. He felt himself sailing back through space. At the same time, he thought he was yelling to the boys, across the encampment some forty or fifty feet, to come help us. We later learned that neither of us uttered a sound.

Roald couldn't breathe. He decided he should stop hollering, because he felt he had only a little breath left and knew he shouldn't waste it, so he held onto it. As he describes it, he started sinking into a pit, a long, reddish-black pit like an elevator shaft with one elevator. He felt he was floating down through this thing. Then he saw the light, but it kept getting smaller and smaller, until only a pinpoint was left. Roald remembers thinking, *Oh, I had better not lose track of that light, because if I do, that will be it.* Suddenly, and bewilderingly, he found himself in a great meadow. He isn't certain whether he was actually in the meadow or hovering over it. The overpowering sense of aloneness came upon him. He explains: "I knew I was in the presence of God. I also knew a big decision was being made as to what would happen to me."

Roald wasn't aware that I had been hit at the same time. Unlikely as it may seem, his experience was identical to mine, in that he, too, began reciting the Twenty-third Psalm.

24

Yea, though I walk through the valley of the shadow of death, I will fear no evil: for thou art with me; thy rod and thy staff they comfort me.

Thou preparest a table before me in the presence of mine enemies: thou anointest my head with oil; my cup runneth over. Surely goodness and mercy shall follow me all the days of my life: and I will dwell in the house of the LORD for ever (Ps. 23:4–6).

Alone with his thoughts and his regrets, Roald kept wondering where the Lord was. "If I'm not on Earth and I am alone, where are *You?*" he recalls asking. "God never showed up," Roald adds, "but I surely felt His presence. Since then I have never doubted that there is a God. It is indescribable how you *know* there is a God."

Then began the bargaining: "Lord, save me long enough to bring up the twins. The boys are too young to be without a father. I promise, Lord, I'll do anything . . ." At that moment, Roald sensed he was back in the tent.

We had brought along a big cookie supply for this camping trip, because the boys had warned me that one of their friends was a cookie lover. As the boys described it to us later, when Roald was thrown back, he landed arms spread out on top of the pink pails of cookies. These were very hard, plastic pails with pearl grey tops. He literally smashed the pails, flattening them out.

When I was struck I bolted back at an angle, and as I shot through the tent I took the flap away, ripping it with my body. I landed in kind of a fetal position, my head on Roald's chest.

Roald's bargaining with God was not unlike mine. He had gone forward at a church service as a child, and now he was reminding God. Sadly, however, Roald's life had been lived with only one thought in mind—making his first million.

Many people say they will go to hell because that is where all their friends are, and they will go there and join them and have a grand time. "From my experience," my husband relates, "you are completely alone. And I realized that if I would not be with the Lord, I would really be forever alone."

When Roald let go of the little bit of air that he felt was all that was left between him and death, his lungs started working. He too was completely paralyzed. Every joint was like a tourniquet causing excruciating pain. Gradually he felt the paralysis lessening a bit—first in his eyes, as he moved them just a little, and then in his mouth, as he tried talking. His first words were instructions to one of the boys. "Pump my legs, get the circulation going." The boys told us they did this, pumping his legs up to his chest, but Roald felt nothing.

At the time of the lightning strike, the boys were in their tent, and they were knocked off their feet. The two boatloads of people who had taken shelter were likewise knocked down by the tremendous jolt that struck the island. They likened it to the percussion following the atomic bomb. When the boys got back on their feet, they saw the fireball roll down the beach into the lake.

Smoke was billowing from our tent, and the

stench of burning flesh filled the air. Our clothes were burning and our skin had turned very dark. We acquired an instant dark, almost black, sun-tan. Everyone was screaming. The two older couples who had taken shelter near us ran up to see if they could help. One man looked into the tattered remains of the tent and became ill. The other man began to run up and down, hysterically screaming, "It's too late, too late!"

But it wasn't too late. God, in His marvelous providence, was going to spare our lives.

CHAPTER 3

There Really Is a God

Near where we had pitched our tents was a bay about six blocks wide and three blocks deep, a good fishing inlet. The island was covered with a thick stand of evergreen trees. It was also very rocky. We now know that rocky country is a good place for lightning to strike.

Later, as news of the lightning strike reached the papers, people came from all over to see the area. Sightseers were greeted by fish floating belly-up in the bay.

Between the trees and the water's edge was a sandy beach extending about forty feet. That is where Roald and the boys had elected to pitch our tents. It was a beautiful campsite. The tent Roald and I occupied was pitched next to a tall, bare pine which you could tell had been struck by lightning in the past. The tree was stripped of its bark. There was another tree nearby. The trees provided good footage for the lines of the tent. It was an umbrella tent with metal posts. We hung our bathing suits and clothes on the umbrella-like spokes. One of the spokes of the umbrella tent had a guide wire which I had my hand on at the time of the strike.

During the screaming and the nightmare that had instantly come upon everyone, a woman, seven months pregnant, and her fifteen-year-old daughter came running up the beach. They, along with her husband and a fishing guide, came from Crawfordsville, Indiana, to Rainy Lake to fish every year. We are convinced God placed her there.

The woman had just completed a course in first aid. She hadn't been instructed on what to do for someone struck by lightning, paralyzed and burning, but she took one look and began to give her daughter instructions. The daughter worked on me and the woman worked on Roald. We were actually suffocating; she couldn't find our pulse. Artificial respiration was needed, and quickly.

In the meantime, the fishing guide and the husband of the woman helping Roald crossed the lake during the storm to get the help of a cruiser. The woman and her daughter continued working on us, and we began to breathe in shallow spasms.

Nerve endings had been destroyed over the biggest part of our bodies, and we were insensitive to touch or feel. Someone raised my head to give me some coffee and someone else said, "Oh don't, it is boiling," but the scalding liquid had already burned my tongue and throat.

As the blood once more started circulating through our bodies, the pain was excruciating. It felt like a part of the body was "awaking from sleep"—first there was numbness, then tingling, which in our case was magnified thousands of times. Our bodies came back to life one area at a time. The paralysis began to break first in the top of our heads. Slowly it broke over the chest region, and then down into our hands.

It took four men to carry Roald to the cruiser; it took two to carry me. Our bodies had become bloated and heavy. They laid us on the floor of the cruiser and began the long forty-mile trek back across the lake to the hospital at International Falls. They continued pouring coffee and brandy into us. We felt nothing. Later the doctor told us if the woman and her daughter had not arrived at that precise moment and begun the resuscitation efforts, we wouldn't have had a chance. The coffee and brandy stimulated our hearts.

It was discovered that the lightning hit Roald in the upper left shoulder by his neck, crossed over through his right hand into me, and shot out my right leg. In so doing, it went across the spinal column. The lightning left a dinner-plate size marking on my back, and marks on my front, down the groin, into my right leg, and down to my ankle.

Roald and I will be forever grateful that faulty judgment on the part of the hospital personnel made it possible for us to be placed in a room together, beside one another in two beds. (In the state of Minnesota, until recently, it was against the law to put a man and woman in the same room, even if married.) But shock had set in, we were both in a terrible mess, our clothing looked like it had been shredded by scissors, and the burns were of such intensity that it was thought we could not possibly live long. So they did not separate us.

I was vaguely conscious of people coming into the room, looking at us, and asking, "Who are they?" Someone would reply, "I don't know, but aren't they strange looking people?" I had blonde hair and Roald had little hair left, and with our very dark skin we must have been quite a spectacle.

As the shock gradually wore off, I was conscious of only one thing—the miracle of being alive. I knew Roald was in a bed next to me, yet the person lying there did not look like him. I was overwhelmed. When I was dying, I had thought it was just me. To realize my husband was lying there in the same condition I was in was too much.

At the same time, consciousness was seeping back into Roald's brain. As it came to him that I had also been struck by lightning, and that I was lying there in a pitiful state, he was just as emotionally distressed as I.

Roald and I had been happily married two years at this time. We had known one another four years prior to marriage. During these six years we had what we thought was the best built-in communication system any man and woman could enjoy. We didn't need other people around to make our joy complete. We often talked until the wee hours of the morning. We had marvelous rapport.

Yet we had never *really* communicated. Not in

the way God intends man and woman to communicate.

That day, as we lay in the two beds, side by side, we looked very good to one another only because we were alive. My husband reached out to touch my hand, and as we touched fingertips and looked at one another, something happened.

My husband dropped the mask that even he was not aware he had been wearing. For the first time in his life he communicated to me in a spiritual sense. And I? I dropped the mask I had not been aware I was wearing, and I, too, communicated with him.

Roald said, "Wilma, there really is a God."

And I replied, "Yes, yes, Roald, I know."

CHAPTER 4

The Miracle of Being Alive

The sound of a thousand freight trains bearing down upon us filled our heads until we thought they would burst. The shrill shriek, like a severe windstorm, whistled through our ears. Both of Roald's eardrums were blown out—one had two big holes, and the other had one big hole. Doctors doubted they would heal. (Three months later they were not only healed but had returned to normal.) Now, however, as Roald and I lay between sheets covered with ointment, we heard each other speak of the miracle of being alive, and shared mutual misery.

The hospital attendants did not try to feed us intravenously; they did little for us, as they did not expect us to live. "There is nothing we can do," we heard them say, "except to leave them wrapped between the sheets of ointment."

Roald felt a great peace come over him. Later we were told we were both in a state of shock. He describes that feeling of peace as like being "in the pocket of God." Roald was praying, for the realization had overwhelmed him that there really is a God.

I looked across at Roald, lying there in intense pain, more dead, it appeared, than alive. Through the earsplitting noise in my head, I cried out, "Roald, I know there really is a God, but I wasn't going to Him!"

Roald looked at me, with the same roaring in his ears, through the agony of his multiple burns, then turned his face to the wall and began to weep. Then I too began to weep. The barriers were down in our relationship as they had never been down before—we who had thought our relationship and communication were so perfect.

"I told God if He let me live I would do anything for Him," I heard Roald say.

"So did I," I responded.

"I was repeating the Twenty-third Psalm," he said.

"Roald, so was I!" I cried out in amazement.

Two things became very clear and were communicated for all time: God *is*, and we never had a problem with that from that time on; and we felt we could safely say that God has plans for every life that comes into this world. Beyond this, our ability to put into words what we had experienced and the impressions it made on our thinking were rather limited. We were not yet perceptive in the things of the Lord.

Back on Rainy Lake Island, the boys were breaking up camp. People came over from International Falls and helped take everything down, then they packed everything and got the boys and the gear back across the water and into a motel. The woman who had saved us and her daughter and husband came to the hospital and gave unstintingly of themselves as they waited to see how we did.

Roald's burns were more severe than mine. The first time I attempted to walk, after the paralysis broke, my legs felt like rubber. After it was apparent we were going to live, we were put into different rooms. When it came time to leave the hospital, the boys brought us back to Minneapolis in the rear of the station wagon. I remember as we were driving home I was thinking it was the softest automobile ride I had ever had. It was like riding on a pillow, floating through the air.

We were placed under a doctor's care in Minneapolis. When I explained the "soft" ride home to him he said it was because our nerve endings had been destroyed, burned off. "What can we expect by way of recovery with that type of nerve damage?" I asked the doctor.

His answer was "I do not know." We were plainly a puzzle to the medical profession. They simply did not understand how we had survived. We all knew that by God's grace our lives had been saved, and that we would be eternally grateful He placed on that island, at that particular time, a woman who knew how to give cardiopulmonary resuscitation.

The *Albuquerque Journal* (October 26, 1978) carried a story about a woman in Greensboro,

North Carolina, who was struck by a bolt of lightning and survived. "I think everybody is surprised that, with a direct strike, she could survive," said Dr. Richard Bloomfield, the physician who was called to the emergency room at Carteret General Hospital in Morehead City shortly after the accident. This doctor said the woman's symptoms were similar to those of victims of cardiac arrest, except for the burns and ruptured eardrums. "Basically, she survived [because] God was with her," he said.

Our doctors had never treated anyone who had survived being struck by lightning. One doctor felt that possibly in three years' time we might regain near-normal hearing and retain only slight nerve damage. A more optimistic doctor remarked that the human body is such a fantastic "machine" that it was capable of repairing damaged nerves in possibly six months to a year.

We now know that the Great Physician thinks far beyond what mere man thinks and can do what mere man with all his ingenuity and medical prowess cannot possibly do. Roald and I were totally healed in three months' time. The nerve-end damage was completely repaired, our burns beautifully healed, and the scars have faded with time.

In more recent years, as I have come to understand the work of the Holy Spirit in an individual's life, I have recognized that we have five spiritual senses that parallel our physical senses. For three months our physical senses were dulled. At first we could not see plainly; in the same way, people have spiritual eyes, and until the truth is revealed, they are blind spiritually. We could not taste or sense when hot coffee and brandy were being poured down our throats. In like manner, we have spiritual taste. The Bible says, "O taste and see that the LORD is good . . ." (Ps. 34:8).

Then there is the sense of smell. Without the ability to smell, you are unable to appreciate a sweet fragrance or an odor that could warn, for instance, of leaking gas. Though smoke might cause your eyes and the tissue within your nose to burn, you would not smell it. The Bible speaks of those who have ". . . an odor of a sweet smell, a sacrifice acceptable, wellpleasing to God" (Phil. 4:18).

After the screaming siren stopped sounding off in our heads, we appreciated more than ever our sense of hearing. Jesus, in speaking to the multitude on the seashore, said: "Who hath ears to hear, let him hear" (Matt. 13:9). When the disciples questioned Him as to why He spoke to the people in parables, He replied, "Therefore speak I to them in parables: because they seeing see not; and hearing they hear not, neither do they understand" (v. 13).

Roald and I were to be like that for ten long years following our experience of being struck by lightning. We were like those whom the Book of Hebrews says are "dull of hearing" (Heb. 5:11). Jesus speaks of sheep who follow Him, "for they know his voice" (John 10:4).

Hanson's disease is a nice way to talk about

leprosy. In biblical times the disease was greatly feared. "Unclean, unclean," the people called out when a leper appeared. Leprosy patients easily become disfigured. One reason for this is they lose their sense of touch. They have no feeling of pain and can be easily burned without realizing it. "Spiritual leprosy" would be a good name for sin.

We could not feel many things in the three months following the lightning strike. We had live-in help and had to be very careful or we could easily have been burned again. When we first tried to hold things, we were like spastics. This is what happens to us spiritually—until we are touched by Jesus; we are beyond feeling and "burn" ourselves with sin all the time.

Here we were, two people who had stood, as it were, on the brink of eternity and had made a vow to the God we knew was there. We were on our feet once again physically, and it was time to pay the vow. "How do you do that?" we asked each other.

CHAPTER 5

Repaying God

I lay awake many nights wondering just how we could best repay God for sparing our lives. Several times I asked Roald "How do you think we should do it? It's not as though we can put an ad in *The Minneapolis Tribune* and expect results."

The masks we had worn in four years of court-ship and two years of marriage were stripped from us as we lay in the hospital like two naked kids. Amazingly, the masks had gone up again after we were healed. But I meant to pay God back, under my own terms.

As we thought it out as best we could, Roald and I thought probably the first thing we should do was join a church. We began making the rounds of some of the city churches with the boys. We finally settled on one that pleased us all and joined it.

I had gone to church in my childhood and adult years, particularly on important "religious" holi-days. Now, suddenly, I was there whenever the doors opened. I became what you might call the original "do-good kid." I just worked up a storm. I was on every committee you can think of. Much as

I hated washing dishes, I washed dishes. I made sandwiches and more sandwiches. I was on the "Board of Religious Education," and I was "adult advisor" for young people, with Roald as coadvisor. But that was not enough.

I then began running around town, volunteering for everything. I got on all the charity boards that would have me. That was not difficult to do, for they all needed volunteers. I was racking up brownie points like crazy, and Roald was equally involved. In the next few years as we would go panting by each other, he would say, "What do you think, honey? You think God is pleased?"

I answered, "I hope so; I'm sure getting tired!"

But I had it all figured out. It was like a pair of scales. On one side I had a very heavy item—the gift of restored life, and let me tell you, that *is* heavy. On the other side, there was me—a wavering and uncertain me. But I needed some weight on that unsteady, wavering side to give some balance. I needed something to even myself out, so there I was, piling all of the good, worthwhile things on the side where I was, so I could gain a degree of balance. I was even hopeful I could tip it a little bit on my behalf. All the while I was hoping a voice would come from somewhere in outer space and say, "Okay, honey, you finally paid Me back. End of script, cut."

It was very faulty communication. Very poor reasoning. A voice was not going to come from outer space, and inwardly I knew it. Still I kept up the awful pace, working harder than ever, never knowing when I had done enough.

At times I had the feeling that inside, behind all the many masks I now donned to suit the various occasions, there was a little creature who had been hiding since year one. No one knew about her. She was me, the real me, inside, in the dark. There were no lights, and there were heavy storm shutters on the windows, and a heavy storm door. Heavy sandbags were piled around the base of the house, and the little creature had peepholes all around, with a gun in each one. She manned the guns daily to keep out anyone who might attempt to get in where she lived.

But in me, where this creature lived in the dark, there were no masks, so she could tell it like it was. This was the honest thought, without the mask, that the little creature had: *Why does work for God have to be so boring? I've got all these years ahead of me to pay God back, and I said I was going to do this, and I'm hung up on all this activity—and I'm so bored! I just have to keep on keeping on like this. Where is all that peace and joy I heard about, that if you are so good you are supposed to experience? I don't have any of it.*

Not only that, but a cold, lonely wind blew through the house inside me every so often, and the little creature would rush around trying to hold the shutters closed, because she knew it was possible to die. She kept wondering, *Have I done enough in case I die now?*

I didn't want anybody to know I was having such thoughts. Around me were people who knew why I was so busily involved, but I refused to acknowledge that they had caught on. Inside I thought, *But it's not fair; it's just not fair.* Deep inside—where that little creature lived—she was very lonely.

Outwardly I always talked it up real good with everybody. But inside was that lonely feeling. Right in the middle of a party or large gathering, I would feel all alone.

I realized I had a lot of unanswered questions, but I tried shrugging the realization off. *Wilma, you've always had lots of questions.* But it bugged me, and I knew I'd always been trying to find something to give my life meaning, to attain a sense of fulfillment. I remembered that even as a child I'd been busy trying to get "life" into my life. I grew up, charging through life, thinking, *If I can do this, or be this, then I will be happy.*

I remembered once wanting a date with a certain boy, and working hard to get that date. I thought if I could just get that date, that would be the ultimate triumph. I got the date, and it was no big deal. Then on to the next thing. I thought if I could just be a drum majorette . . . I became one, and it took a lot of practice. But even the best of drum majorettes drops the baton now and then.

Although I had not verbalized it, I had thought in my subconscious, *Someday, if I can just meet the man of my dreams, someone I can really love, then I will get married and I will be like a fairy princess, living happily ever after.* I met the man I thought I loved, and I did love him very much, and yet it was *not* the living-happily-ever-after situation I had hoped for. The lonely, restless feelings persisted, and I could not even share them with the man of my dreams.

After five years of hectic activity, Roald and I had the marvelous opportunity to adopt an adorable, eight-day-old baby girl. (The doctors had told me I would be unable to bear children.) I held that little girl in my arms, and it seemed for a time that I had finally found the answer. I was fulfilled, diapers and all. The problem was, it lasted only three months.

The baby was crying. I got up to go to her. The distance between our bedroom and the nursery was not long. All of a sudden, a lonely wind, like a sneak attack, blew through the house inside me where the little creature lived. The creature started rushing around trying to hold the shutters closed to keep the feelings out. The overwhelming realization swept over me: *Even having this beautiful, darling baby isn't where it's at.* Something was still missing. I thought, *Oh phooey, I thought I had found the answer.*

I gave myself a little pep talk: *Having a baby is a wonderful thing. Now you have the perfect excuse to extricate yourself from all the frenzied activity you've unwittingly gotten yourself into.* I decided to get out of some of my work without losing face, if I possibly could. So I took my excuse and dropped off a number of committees and charities, still staying on enough things to "look good." Now I could stay home and be a "good mother."

Then I encountered another problem. I had too much time to think. It wasn't long before I couldn't stand that, so I started getting baby-sitters. This time I was off in pursuit of knowledge.

If you can just cram enough knowledge in the house where the little creature lives, she will quiet down and you can feel warm and cozy, I told myself. You name it, I probably studied it, read about it, or took a course in it during the five years that followed. I took every positive thinking and self-improvement course I could find. I studied the religions of the world, Eastern mysticism, and philosophy. I found absolutely nothing to give the little creature that fully satisfied her. I found a lot to clutter up the little house inside me, but nothing of real worth.

I remember listening to a record by a comedienne who does a marvelous takeoff on a little girl named Edith. Edith is five and a half years old. In one part of the record, Edith is walking home with a lady. She takes the lady's hand and says, "Lady, do you know God can see you, lady?"

The lady replies, "He can?"

"Yes, yes, He can. He has a TV set, you know. He is there, and He can see you," Edith says.

The lady looks at this precocious child and says, "Is that so, Edith!"

"Yes, you know, lady, whenever I think He is watching, you know what I do? I always sing and dance and do a little commercial for myself," Edith testifies.

In moments of being honest with myself, I had to admit I was like little Edith. "Hey God, look at me. I am really good. See how good I am! I am doing all these great things for You. I really deserve to go to heaven, God."

I now know how many there are who sing, dance, and do little commercials for themselves through life in vain efforts to impress God.

CHAPTER 6

Strike One!

I had the uncomfortable feeling God was not particularly impressed with me or my efforts to repay Him. Often I reflected on my childhood and my father. He was a very simple person, but he had a great prayer life. My memories of my father are tied together with his persistent praying and consistent faithfulness in seeing that my younger brother and I attend Sunday school and church.

I had been exposed to the truths of the Bible in those growing-up years. I began to think of my life in terms of a ballgame. The teachings about God and Jesus left me without excuse—I could never say I had not heard about this Son of God who hung on the cross for the sins of the world. *Wilma,* something in me said, *you struck out as a child.*

Strike two was being struck by lightning. Would there be some kind of a third strike? Would I miss the pitch then, too?

My parents divorced when I was six. For a time my brother and I lived with Daddy's sister in Vancouver, Washington. Daddy came to see us only on weekends. The days in between were long, lonely, and sad.

I missed my mother, too. She was a beautiful but vain woman. Though we did not receive much love from her, still she was our mother.

Hate began to build up within me. I saw my little brother turn into a crybaby. You either hate or cry when you're hurt. I then took it upon myself to be my brother's protector. I became hardened and began to hide my true feelings. I turned inward. During my years from ages six to twelve, we lived with various people. Those were difficult years.

Evangelist Billy Graham was appearing in Portland, Oregon, in those days. A golfing partner convinced my father to attend a couple of the meetings with him. As Daddy related it, he steeled himself against the desire to go forward. Daddy was forty-nine at the time.

We moved to Camas, Washington. Dad's friend convinced my father to go with him to hear another visiting evangelist. This time my father took my brother and me along. That night, Dad's friend put his arm around my father's shoulder and said, "Jim, Jesus loves you." I remember this, for my father told me, but it did not communicate to me as it did to Daddy. Dad walked forward that night and committed his life to Christ. My little brother and I tagged down the aisle behind him, not understanding. After that, we were *really* in Sunday school and church. Before this, Daddy would drop us off, but now our lives were drastically changed. My father became a completely committed man. He began to pray for us, his children. Those prayers were to continue without letup for thirty years. If this book does nothing else, let it pay tribute to a praying father!

During those years after my father became a Christian, I became argumentive and stubborn. My hatred continued to build. I was full of resentment but covered it up with an air of superiority in my continual efforts to achieve. As I grew older, and as I walked away from the church, I began reading things not fit for human consumption and making new friends who were not associated with the church. I became agnostic in my lifestyle.

Inwardly, however, I was a puzzled person. Questions surfaced frequently, only to be shoved into my subconscious. Who am I really? Where did I come from? Aside from the biological facts, why am I here and where am I going? Is there really a God? If I die, will I live again? Is there a world beyond this world? Is there really a place called heaven? Questions. All kinds of questions. But I erected my facade and continued the trivial chatter with my new friends.

When I was thirteen, I saw my mother once, briefly. She pulled up in front of our house in a huge limousine. To me it looked like it stretched out a block. I was greatly impressed. She brought my brother and me ice cream. She was still beautiful. Because of my great need for a mother, even though I really hated her, I gave her my affection, and I began to write letters to her after that. I would dream about her at night. Then I had spells when I was angry, and I would decide I'd never write her again. Now and then she answered my letters—with short notes.

The next time I saw my mother I was sixteen. She had another husband. She asked me to live with her in Portland. I jumped at the chance. It lasted three months. It was a traumatic time, and I could hardly wait to get back to Daddy. I did not see her again until I was twenty-five and my first marriage was ending.

One day I came home from high school and told my father I was going to become a fashion model. My first job was modeling hats. I would go to the Portland department stores and model new lines that were being shown by the buyers. I made a commission on the hats I modeled that sold well. I was not quite five-feet-five-inches, but I walked tall and carried myself well. All the while I was living in a fantasy world.

In this fantasy world my mother was very loving, and she was always there when I needed her most. Of course, she was more beautiful than any other girl's mother. This mother cared for me. When I was asked about my home life, I would weave fantastic tales about our fabulous family. Thus began a pattern of dishonesty.

As I started getting jobs, I began to lie about my age. I thought nothing of adding a few years to my age to land a certain job. I'd think, *Wasn't that slick? You really pulled that off well!*

I developed a form of self-confidence that was a

false front to cover my many insecurities. A girl friend and I actually had the audacity to walk into a very large publicity agency in New York City, and I sold myself as a writer. It was a romantic-sounding job—I was to go to Portugal. I bluffed my way all the way, even to writing a *resume* on myself. At the last minute my courage gave out, and I gave some flimsy excuse as to why I couldn't accept the job after all.

At age twenty I met an officer who said he could not live without me. He was going to go overseas and said he might get killed, so he insisted I marry him! It was ridiculous. My friends thought he was the most handsome man they had ever laid eyes on, but I didn't especially care for him—he was conceited, in my estimation.

But I was flattered by all his attention, and I was vulnerable. "I am going to get killed" impressed me, and I thought, *If I can make him happy, then I should marry him. It's the least I can do for him and my country.* Not only that, my closest friend married his good friend. I felt she deserted me when she moved to the officer's quarters with her new husband. She was going to the officer's club, and I thought, *How glamorous, and here I am, and he wants to marry me. I could be living like that, too.*

I was shallow, immature, and a phony. I did tell him, "I don't love you," and I seemed to get a lot of satisfaction out of that. But he said, "That's all right, Wilma, I still want you to marry me." I did.

50

Within three months he went overseas. Yes, I was living in the officers' quarters and my life was more glamorous. But I was one unhappy young married woman. My father had tried to talk me out of this marriage, but I would not listen. At the end of fifteen months, when my husband returned from overseas, we moved to Detroit.

Certain members of my husband's family were well known in political circles. I was twenty-one, and this lifestyle was new to me. I began to be very lonely for my father. The marriage could only be characterized as unwise. We had a bad time of it.

By now I was an Arthur Murray dance instructor. Earlier, I also had a stint as a department store window designer. I found I could bluff my way through almost anything. My husband owned drugstores, and I managed one store for a while. I continued doing some modeling and sold furs and women's exclusive apparel.

The eventual breakup of our marriage those many years ago was the same as the breakup in marriages today. When you do not have Jesus Christ as the center of your life, and your marriage is shaky, you are headed for trouble.

I realize now that one of the things that propelled me into an early marriage was my feeling of rejection by my mother. My imagination ran rampant, and as I saw girl friends marrying servicemen, I began to fear I was being rejected by a lot of people. There had to be something unworthy in me. I now understand all that happened, as I see it from the perspective of being a Christian.

A columnist wrote that today revenge is regarded as a predictable—even reasonable—response to the unforgivable crime of "malparenting." In recent times we have seen new books written about famous women who were also mothers—books written by their rejected daughters. These mothers became walking targets for the poisoned pens of their daughters, each of whom seems to have lain in waiting to pounce.

Christina Crawford's *Mommie Dearest* shows her mother, Joan Crawford, to have been pathologically abusive to her adopted daughter. Sadly, Christina was not able to see her mother in any context other than that of her own emotional pain and the unmet needs of her own life.

I have asked God to forgive me for the feelings of ill will I harbored for so many years toward my mother. I was one-dimensional in viewing her. But I can go on record now as stating God is the Healer and the Remover of all bitterness. The last time I saw my mother, in 1968, I told her, "Mother, I love you and want to thank you just for carrying me in your womb." I had nothing but love for her, total compassion. God wipes and washes the slates of our lives clean. God has said to me "Wilma, you are the person I am dealing with. You are forgiven. Now leave your mother to Me." And that's what I have done.

It is important to recognize we are all survivors of our childhoods. We cannot have much control over what happens to us as children. We become products, to a large extent, of what was done for us and to us. I now see that. I understand and therefore need not harbor revenge. Someone has said revenge is the weapon of the eternal child. The Bible tells us to put away childish things when we are adults (see 1 Cor. 13:11).

We fashion our lives out of the history of our past. I struck out as a child and as an unwise young adult. When the reality of God's existence became clear to me, the volatile mixture of my emotions, combined with my past, produced a driven women. I needed a stabilizing force in my life.

CHAPTER 7

My Hidden Fear

C. S. Lewis said in *Mere Christianity*, "If I find in myself a desire which no experience in this world can satisfy, the most probable explanation is that I was made for another world." The first time I read that, it hit me squarely between the eyes. That is what is within everyone—a desire that the world cannot satisfy, no matter how happily married a person might be, no matter how successful a person may become, no matter how well things are going.

Today everyone is interested in communication, which is often dependent upon the vehicle of words. If you attempt to communicate with someone and you do not have the same definitions, no matter how long you dialogue, you are not really communicating. Communication has become very important to me. I have made the marvelous discovery that a Christian is a person who is convinced that the fact of Christ is the plainest clue to the meaning of things.

I ran away from the reality of Christ as a child and as a young woman, but the "Hound of

Heaven" was ever in pursuit. Communication with my second husband, Roald, took on a new dimension for a brief period following our being struck by lightning, but in our busy efforts to repay God, we lost something in transition.

Following the accident, I kept it a secret from everyone, including Roald, that I now had a great, overwhelming fear. I had not been fearful of death before the lightning struck. Actually, I never thought of death as happening to *me*—it was always for someone else. Now it was constantly in the back of my mind, hovering like an unwelcome intruder.

I even became afraid to fly. We went on vacations with friends to Acapulco. We had been doing this for some time. Roald had a very successful company. In recent years, when I was introduced as a speaker at business functions, it was said that my husband was chairman of the board of the National Vitamin Corporation. Frequently the person making the introductions would say, "That is why Wilma looks so good, even with keeping a heavy schedule and having ten grandchildren." When I acknowledged the introduction, I would find myself saying, "Thank you. You know, I don't think I have been communicating too well with you. You have assumed I have been dipping into my husband's products and that is what makes me so healthy. As a matter of fact, my husband makes a fine product for horses and cows."

The business prospered, affording us many opportunities for interesting trips. I could not open up to Roald and communicate my hidden fear of death, so I had to find a way for us to fly in which I wouldn't be constantly thinking, *What if we crash and are killed!* I solved that problem by imbibing. I was restless until the stewardess brought drinks. I tried making jokes about it and felt I was fooling everyone. My problem was fear and I needed a crutch.

People say today, "I do not see how you could respond the way you did to God for ten years. How come it took that long? After all, you made that promise to God."

There is what I call bogus faith. Such fraudulent faith has a faulty foundation. When you hit some-one's knee, his lower leg reacts. As soon as you stop hitting the knee, it stops jumping. It is a reflex action. Bogus faith is like that. The root of that kind of faith is fear. When you are faced with some kind of crisis, there is the reflex action of remembering, "Oh yes, there is a God. He is my Creator. I bet He could help me right now." Your faith sparks for a moment, thinking, *He can save me.* The moment the crisis is past, it is back to the old stand again. This is so common.

I can take people through crises in their lives and show them how we all do this. It is hard for us to face up to a miracle. A lot of people are healed, but they do not like to face up to what that means. God does things all the time for us, but we do not admit it. Facing up meant something was going to be required of me, and I wanted to pay Him back in my own way, with *my* work, on *my* terms. My self was going to stay intact. I genuinely wanted to pay Him back, but it had to be my own way. I saw nothing wrong in that.

If people tried to talk to me about the accident, or I was reminded in some way, I had to think fast to switch the subject. The fear of death haunted me all the time. In order to cover this I lived fast, I moved fast, and worked fast and hard. I see people doing it all the time. I was like that—I didn't want to have time to stop and think.

CHAPTER 8

Struck by Love

"Wilma, I'd like to invite you to a luncheon. It's at your club." My neighbor did not belong to our country club, so I thought, *What can be going on at the club that I don't know anything about?*

I asked her that very question.

"Well, it is something new in our area, Wilma, and I think you'll really enjoy it. It's called Christian Women's Club."

My response was "I've never heard of it."

"Well, you have now," she replied with a laugh. "How about it? I've even got a baby-sitter for you."

Mentally I was clicking off my whole arsenal of excuses for occasions such as this, but suddenly I stopped. The little creature inside had a thought—inside, where she tells it like it is. *Well, I might as well say yes to her and get her off my back. Chances are if it's at my club it can't be too religious.*

That was some thought, wasn't it, for a woman who had supposedly been giving her life to God for ten years! But it was what I really thought. My neighbor, who had been inviting me patiently to various functions for two years, and had always gotten some kind of weak excuse for an answer, suddenly heard me say "Okay."

When I walked into that club with my neighbor a few days later, I was fervently manning the guns inside the creature's little house. With my faulty communication system, I had it all figured out. I was supposedly already a Christian, you understand—I was known for doing all these good things, and I belonged to a big church and the best clubs. I had been baptized, catechized, confirmed, and the whole bit. So I walked in with my guard up.

I was all set to deal with the "pickle noses" and the "little buns of hair," and their "uptight propositions." I knew nobody could possibly have any fun with a bunch of women like that, and I wanted no part of it. I had all kinds of little "goodies" in my life that I wanted to hang on to so I could continue to have fun. True, I wasn't having any fun, but I might have fun some day. I wanted to be ready when "some day" came—so that day I was ready for the inevitable, and I thought, *Just don't anyone rock my boat!*

To my amazement, I came into a room full of lovely ladies, and there wasn't a "pickle nose" in the crowd. The first thing that happened was that I won the door prize! I had never won anything before in my life. That blew my mind. The food was excellent and the music great. I began to relax. I relaxed so much that by the time the speaker got up, I just leaned back and prepared to enjoy whatever she was going to share. She opened her mouth and began communicating the most exciting thing, the most wonderful news that I had ever had the privilege of hearing.

People always had difficulty communicating with me. Oh, they didn't know it—I was very clever at disguising boredom and disinterest in what was going on about me. Recently, I read about a new electronic gadget that decreases the sound waves in a given area. Let's say you want some "sack time," but the children are making a lot of noise. You take the gadget, hang it over your bed, turn the volume up, and right where you are, you have a little, quiet zone. As I read about it, I thought, *That is pretty neat, but it's really nothing new. I've had one of those built into my system for years, and I've kept it in good repair and with the volume up most of the time.* It is amazing what you can avoid hearing that way.

That day I must have forgotten to turn the volume up, or my "system" had broken down, because the speaker came through loud and clear. "Do you know that God loves you so much that had you been the only person who ever lived, God would have sent His Son, Jesus Christ, to die on the cross for you? And Christ loves you so much that He would have volunteered to come and pour out His blood on the cross so that you might live eternally, so that you might have life and have it more abundantly, right now, today. Did you know that?"

I stared at the attractive young woman speaking. She continued, "I didn't know that for years." Then she shared her life story. She talked about the little thoughts she had had in her inner being where she was so lonely, and how she had always been trying to find something to satisfy her inner being. One day someone communicated the fact to her that "Christianity is not a church; Christianity is not all of those good, wonderful, fine, needful, worthwhile things that we do; but Christianity is a Person—it is Jesus Christ."

I identified.

Simple identification because of a simple communication of truth. Life-changing truth. I listened as she explained that God's plan for every one of us is for us to reach out and receive the free gift He offers us. "We cannot earn it, we cannot join enough churches, we cannot do enough good things to merit it—it is a gift and God said, 'Just hold out your hand and receive what I want to give you.' "

The little creature inside me lapped up every word. I was sitting on the edge of my seat. This was too good to be true. But this speaker was saying it was true. "Jesus says that, to as many as will receive Him, He will give the right, the authority, the power, the ability to become His child. Christ said that He came so that we might have life, and that we might have it more abundantly.

Jesus said, 'I am the way, the truth, and the life: no man cometh unto the Father, but by me' [John 14:6]."

At that point I realized why I had not been able to get near the Father ten years before. I had not known the Good Shepherd. I only knew *about* Him and never realized God intended that I know Him personally as the living, resurrected Lord. When the speaker that day talked of Jesus as being the "Good Shepherd," and quoted John 10:11, "I am the good shepherd: the good shepherd giveth his life for the sheep," I had no trouble envisioning Him that way. Jesus said in that same passage He was "the door: by me if any man enter in, he shall be saved . . ." (v. 9).

I heard her say, "Behold, I stand at the door, and knock: if any man hear my voice, and open the door, I will come in to him, and will sup with him, and he with me" (Rev. 3:20). I felt and heard Him knocking. "Lay down your do-it-yourself kit, Wilma. Open the door to that inner sanctum of self, and I will come in, and I will give you what you have been looking for—life, abundant life, joy and peace. '. . . Not as the world giveth, give I unto you. Let not your heart be troubled, neither let it be afraid' " (John 14:27).

At that moment, as this young woman continued to speak of the living Christ, I had a vision of who I had missed on that trip ten years before. I realized I was hearing truth. I thought, *This is it. It is so simple. It is a gift, but man constantly misses the mark.*

Then I heard her say, "This is what sin is—missing the mark. God had a plan for the world, but sin entered the scene. 'For all have sinned, and come short of the glory of God' [Rom. 3:23]. The glory of God is the plan He has for *your* life." I knew she was talking to me.

"I am going to say a little prayer about you, and all you need do is invite Christ into your heart with an act of your will." She explained we are tripartite beings—that we have intellect, emotions, and a will. I could understand that. Intellectually, I understood the facts about Christ, but I never understood He was actually God come in the flesh.

Emotionally I felt good about Christ—especially on Good Friday between noon and three. You could find me in church crying at Eastertime because they crucified Him, not knowing He had died for *me*. But with my *will*, I had never surrendered to Him or trusted Him with the reins of my life. This is where we get to the nitty-gritty.

"Christ wants to come in and give you answers to the questions you have and the questions your children are asking. Christ wants to come in and give you a love for that neighbor you wish you could love more. Christ wants to come in right at your point of need and give you solutions that you have been seeking," she said. I knew I could no longer resist.

I knew I needed to know a lot more, but as best I knew how, I invited Christ to come into my life that moment, and I trusted Him with my future.

Outwardly nothing seemed to happen, *but my whole life changed.*

I don't have a frightened little creature living inside me any longer. Nor do I have a spooky little house with a cold wind blowing through. He is God, and He is exactly who He says He is. He came into my life in 1966, and if ever I have written the truth, I am writing it now. I have never had a bored moment since then, not one. If I thought I was busy before, I was standing still. If you depend upon any other vehicle to get you where God is, other than Jesus Christ and what He has done for you on the cross, you will never make it.

That day I was *struck by love.* It was the love of Christ that broke and cracked me. That love fractured the hard shell around my heart.

CHAPTER 9

I Am Not Ashamed of You

I now know that for years I fought against the reality of Christ because of my lifestyle. God wants to be number one in a person's life, and when an individual finally succumbs to an acknowledgment of who He is, and who His Son is, then that person yields to God. But I wanted no part of it. I feared it would demand more than I was willing to give up. Recognition of His irresistible love had never come to me—never until that unforgettable day, when I was drawn by God's love as I heard about it at a Christian Women's Club luncheon.

As I sat in that lovely clubhouse dining room, I knew I was going to cry. In that room were a lot of women I knew. I had never let anyone break through my mask. My old habits were deeply ingrained. Quickly I started bargaining with the Lord. *Look, God, wait until I get home. Don't make a fool out of me in front of all these women. When I get home I'll talk to You about all of this.* But deep inside, in that way I have since come to recognize as God speaking, I heard Him say, *This is it, Wilma.*

Suddenly all the times flashed before me when I'd had the opportunity to accept Him but would not listen. Now I could no longer resist Him. It became easier to say *yes* and give in than to fight the love of the Holy Spirit that was sweeping through my entire being.

When I won the door prize earlier, I had taken the box of beautiful table mats and along with my purse had leaned them nearby against a pillar. My neighbor was seated behind me. The speaker was really getting to me, and my sunglasses were in my purse. I didn't have a handkerchief or tissue in my hands, and I desperately needed them. My purse was way back of me, and I was sitting there going crazy—tears streaming down my face, my nose running.

When the speaker said, "Bow your head with me and let's pray together," I pleaded with God. *Oh please Lord, just let me wait until I get home.*

But He was not waiting!

The moment I bowed my head, my nose ran more than ever! I quietly reached for the napkin lying beside my plate and started blotting my face ever so carefully, all the while silently praying with the speaker.

When the woman finished speaking, without turning around so my neighbor Joan could see my face, I leaned back in my chair, almost tipping over in the process. I was determined to get my purse and sunglasses so no one would see my red eyes. (Oh, the pride of womankind!)

Success! I actually managed to reach my purse. Still with my back to Joan, I put my sunglasses on. Then I turned around and said to Joan, "Oh, that was very nice." She said, "You enjoyed it?" I quickly began saying "Hello" to others and nodding to people I knew. I did not want to talk with Joan too much at that point for fear she'd read me—I knew my mask had slipped a bit.

The speaker said if we prayed the prayer with her, we should do ourselves a favor and share it with her. "Leave your name-tag at the door with me. I'll know what you mean, and I want to meet you."

To myself I had said, *No way will I share my name-tag.* I was smiling at people, but conversation was going on in my head. Never had anything like this happened to me before. I was not certain how to handle it and maintain my dignity and composure.

That voice deep inside was saying, *Take the name-tag off. This is the new boss of your life, speaking from the headquarters of your heart. This is the first order of the day.*

Inwardly I responded: *I can't do it, I have my pride, you know. I know women in this room. I have gone to church and have been "Mrs. Church" for years. I don't want them to know I am just now a real Christian.*

Then it was like He said to me: *Don't be ashamed of Me, Wilma. I am not ashamed of you.*

I wiggled the pin out of my name-tag, dropped

the tag in my hand and wadded it up, all the time talking and acting nonchalant. My neighbor Joan, however, saw everything I did. (I still thought I was being so clever.) I walked by Eunice Nethery, the speaker, and took her hand, passing her my crumpled name tag. "It has been very nice," I said, but my eyes pleaded, "Don't give me away."

Eunice took my hand, closed her hand over my name-tag, and responded "I'm so glad," and never gave me away. But Joan saw it all and was certain I had handed my name-tag to Eunice. Joan and I walked out into the brilliant sunshine, and I made light chit-chat. I remember only trivial conversation. Inwardly I was crying out, *Oh, let's hurry and get home*. We picked up our children (my daughter was five years old at the time).

When Joan dropped me off at the house, I leaned over and said, "Now it's my turn. I'll take you to one of my charity luncheons real soon." Somehow my little girl and I got into the house as I fumbled with keys. Behind the sunglasses my eyes were blurry, and the tears were already spilling over. I ran upstairs, way up to the fifth level of our big house. I threw myself down by the bed and let the tears fall. There was such release as they poured out. I was torn through and through. When it was all over and the river of tears had slowed to a slight trickle, I blew my nose, blotted my face and got up. *Well, that is that*, I said to myself. *You certainly got emotional about all this.* Then I said out loud: "Dinner, Ugh!" Making

68

dinner after being out for lunch has never been one of my favorite things to do.

I repaired my makeup and went slowly back down the stairs. I said nothing to my husband about the matter. The mask was back on and fitting snugly by the time he came home.

The next morning I awoke, and as I started to get up, something in my head said, *You did "that."* I then thought, *Oh, you just got emotional yesterday.* I got out of bed, and though you have heard it so often, and it sounds trite, it really happened to me. I looked out the window where there was a large oak tree. It was so beautiful I thought I could not stand it. The tree was magnificent in its early spring splendor. I remembered it was April 1. Then I heard a bird. Everything was in technicolor in a new way I could not describe. I did not understand what had happened, but I now know. The power of the Holy Spirit is real.

CHAPTER 10

Strictly Secret Service

In "The Sound of Music" there is a song that says when you start to read, it is ABC, and when you start to count, it is one, two, and three. When you start to sing it is do-re-mi. You do not start backward on any of this. There is a starting point, and you work from A to Z, not Z to A. My question at this juncture in my life was *Where do I begin?*

I knew I had a lot to learn.

We are body, soul, and spirit. But we reverse the order. God says spirit, soul, and body. When you start to believe, it has to begin in the spirit. Communication has its beginnings in the inner man. Very often we begin with the body, then move to the soulish part—the intellect, our emotions. When Roald and I lay on those two beds in the hospital room, for the first time we were having spiritual communication.

When an individual starts to believe, it starts in the spirit, then permeates the soul, and eventually expresses itself through the body. Romans 10:10 expresses it so well: "for with the heart man believes, resulting in righteousness, and with the mouth he confesses, resulting in salvation" (NASB).

In our relentless ten-year search for God, and in our futile efforts to pay Him back for sparing our lives, we neglected that which could have given us so much of help and hope. Our inner man craved that which God alone can supply. It comes to us from His written Word. Jeremiah speaks of this need and the fulfillment he found. "Thy words were found and I ate them, And Thy words became for me a joy and the delight of my heart" (Jer. 15:16, NASB).

In that same chapter, God speaks to the prophet and tells him He will restore him. "Before Me you will stand; And if you extract the precious from the worthless, You will become My spokesman" (v. 19, NASB).

I knew none of this, but I knew there was more to life and living than Roald and I had experienced. I had tasted something at the luncheon that was sweet, and my spirit wanted more of that which was precious.

The first morning after the luncheon, I could hardly wait for Roald to leave for his office. I had an overwhelming desire to see if I could find some of the verses in the Bible that Eunice Nethery had quoted. I had to find the Bible. It is a terrible confession to have to make, but make it I must. During all those years of serving on the Board of Religious Education in our church, I did not use the Bible.

Now I began to search for it. *Where in the world is it?* I asked myself, as I continued to search throughout the house. Then I began to get embarrassed.

It has got to be around here somewhere, I told myself. I had walked down the aisle with one at my second marriage. It was a little white one with streamers hanging down. Daddy had given it to me.

After a good bit of searching, I finally found the Bible in a drawer in the guest bedroom. That must have made me think this would be a good place to "hide out," for in those days of desperate searching for something to satisfy the early awakenings in my inner spirit, I secluded myself in the guest bedroom. In the middle of the day, while Roald was at the office and my little girl in school or at play, I would pull the drapes, turn on the lamps, and sit there reading the Bible hours on end.

I started reading Daniel. Why, I do not know. And I understood it. I had no problem at all. Never before could I understand the Bible. A couple of times during those ten years I had thought, *I wonder if I still know the Twenty-third Psalm. How come I knew it so well when I was dying?*

The first time I had that thought after inviting Christ into my life, I tried to find the passage and had trouble finding the Psalms in the Bible. When I found it, I thought, *That is strange, for I certainly don't know it now like I remembered it then.*

I got out of Daniel eventually and decided to venture into the New Testament. I had a fantastic time reading it. I could not put it down. I read it and reread it. When it was time for Roald or my little daughter, Marlisa, to come home, I would reluctantly put the Bible back in the drawer, turn out the lights, open the drapes, and leave the room. This continued for several weeks, and I began to grow spiritually.

Roald was important to me. The Lord was at work in my heart and life, but Roald had always been number one. Our lifestyle was important to him. I was fearful of what would happen if he discovered what I was doing. How would he feel if he knew what had happened to me that day at the Christian Women's Club luncheon?

My relationship with Christ at that point was strictly "secret service."

CHAPTER 11

The Number One Man in My Life

When I first met Roald, I was intrigued with his marvelous personality. Humanly speaking, he had many fine traits I would have liked to emulate.

Roald, on the other hand, saw things in me that he needed and liked. This made for a good situation, in that we were opposites, and opposites attract. But we were similar in that we shared the same thoughts about life and living. Our goals were much the same.

We expressed ourselves differently, however. I was outgoing; Roald was shy and introverted. I have always been considered an extrovert.

Roald was an accomplished man. He was president of National Vitamin Products when I met him in 1949. The business was in its infancy, but his accomplishments in manufacturing livestock feeds and formulas were well known in the industry. His time and labor-saving devices had been a source of interest to his family and business acquaintances for years. For many years Roald had an "experimental farm" called Vine Hill, which was a showplace in experimental feeding. College

and university classes were brought there to look
and learn. One of Roald's formulas started a new
era in the feeding of baby animals. It was the first
formula that completely replaced the mother animal's milk in raising baby calves. The product,
called "Calvita," won international fame.

I was tremendously impressed with Roald when
I met him, and my respect for him has never
diminished. We had established a mutually re-
spectful, deeply loving relationship. Both of us
had known the heartache of unhappy first marriages and didn't want a repetition of that. Was it
any wonder I was troubled about his reaction to
my encounter once again with the reality of God?
This time, in contrast to our being struck by lightning and the realization that God was real, I was
now confronted with the reality of His Son.

I worried how Roald would react to this. I loved
him too much to risk losing him. The torment of
loving Jesus and loving my husband but not being
able to share Jesus with him was almost more than
I could stand.

I was a secret service Christian for about six
weeks. But one day I got careless and left the
Bible out of the guest bedroom. My neighbor Joan
had been dropping books off for me to read—I still
had not shared with her what had happened that
day at the luncheon. But she continued to drop by.
One day she said, "Wilma, I've just finished reading this. I think you might enjoy it."

No sooner was she out of the house than I

grabbed the book and devoured it. It was *World Aflame* by Billy Graham. Joan continued to do things like this, and after she'd leave I'd have this overwhelming feeling and think, *I love her. What is the matter with me? Why don't I tell her what happened?* At times my love for Joan was so powerful, I felt like I was going to melt. My gratitude for what she had done in taking me to that luncheon was beyond measure. But my pride was still there.

One day, after Joan had left behind a few books, I'd left the Bible out on the kitchen desk where I'd been reading. Roald came home and asked, "Honey, what has happened to you?"

"What do you mean?" I replied. I was running scared.

"You are just sort of different lately," he answered.

"How?" I questioned him.

"Are you reading the Bible?"

"Yeah. Is there anything wrong with it?" I managed to reply.

"No, but I just wondered."

Inside a voice said, *Tell him what you have done.* "Roald, you know that luncheon I went to a few weeks ago with Joanie?"

"Oh, I think I remember. You weren't so fond about going to that. In fact, as I recall, you were really upset," he said. Roald was remembering our many conversations prior to that time about our neighbors. Sipping our martinis together, we would laugh at our neighbors' attempts at what we called "trying to save us." Roald would tell me, "I think Darrell next door is trying to 'save me,' Wilma," and we'd laugh.

Roald and I were basically not happy. We were happy with each other, and we had the best kind of marriage you can have without Jesus, but we both knew something was missing. We just did not know what it was, or should I say, who it was. While we laughed at our neighbors' efforts to "save us," inwardly we knew it wasn't a laughing matter.

I knew what Roald was thinking. Now I hesitated as I said to him, "Well, that day when I went to the luncheon with Joanie, I heard a woman speak, and I think I became a Christian."

"What do you mean, you became a Christian?" he said, staring at me in amazement. "Wilma, we *are* Christians!"

"Well, I asked Jesus to come into my heart," I replied.

"Didn't you ever do that before? I did when I was a little boy, about eight years old, I think. I remember a visiting evangelist came to the church and he said, 'Come forward if you want to receive Christ,' and I went forward."

I looked at Roald and responded, "I think I did that too, with my dad when I was about twelve years old. I remember following him down the aisle when he went forward—but it didn't mean anything then."

"Oh, I meant it," Roald said. "But good for you, honey, good for you. I'm glad. That's great. You are a good wife, but lately you are better than ever."

I was immensely relieved. There, I'd broken the ice, so to speak, on the subject. I breathed a sigh of relief. But the subject quickly changed.

My desire for Roald to know what I knew and what I was discovering from my reading grew. I instinctively felt Roald did not know the reality I knew. What he knew was just not the same. Yet I could not refute what he had said.

Then the desire to communicate with my darling stepdaughter, Saza, began to take root. We were very close, about thirteen years apart in age, and the best of friends, in addition to the stepmother-stepdaughter relationship. But I was afraid she'd reject what had happened to me, so I remained silent.

The Holy Spirit in me was convicting me of the need to tell my neighbor what had happened and to be upfront and honest with my husband and other family members. The reason I know about the reality of the Holy Spirit is because in those early days of learning from the Bible, He was my only Teacher.

I looked at Roald and loved him with a whole new dimension of love. Roald sensed it. Still, I did not understand it.

Meanwhile, Joan noticed the change in me, too. She was certain she knew what I had done that day at the luncheon, but inwardly she was grieving, for I had not shared it with her. She called a friend and asked, "What shall I do?" and shared what had transpired.

Neighbors and friends began praying for me. All of them gave Joanie the same advice: "Leave her alone. The way you have described her, if she is really that way, she will resent it if you approach her and ask her."

The Holy Spirit was ministering to Joan and to her concerned Christian friends as well. Joanie had told them I seemed cold and contained, yet there was something different. Together she and her praying friends decided that if the Holy Spirit was real in my life and, indeed, if I had asked Christ into my heart, that He would show. They felt the day would come when I would break down and tell Joan what had happened. Sure enough, that day did come.

CHAPTER 12

From Upside Down to Rightside Up

My favorite cartoon strip is good ol' Charlie Brown and the *Peanuts* characters. Charlie is neat. He is *always* going to throw the ball that will win the game! That incredible optimism appeals to me.

In a particular strip I really like, Charlie is at the pitcher's mound. He lets fly with a ball that is hit with such impact by the batter that the ball comes back and hits ol' Charlie right in the solar plexis. It flips him upside down and he stands there, on the pitcher's mound, on his head. Charlie is in trouble. Schroeder is the catcher, and he notes the problem. He leaves his station and comes up to Charlie and says, "Don't feel bad, Charlie Brown. It was a good hit; they made first, second, third. It is a homer, Charlie Brown!"

Charlie just says, "I am upside down; I am upside down!"

No communication. Schroeder just leaves and goes back to his post.

There Charlie Brown stands, on his head. Then the outfielder leaves her post and comes up to

Charlie Brown. "Charlie Brown, Freida is having a party today after the game, and you are invited."

"But I'm upside down; I'm upside down!" Charlie cries.

"That's nice," she says, and goes back to her position.

Then there is the old, trusty beagle, Snoopy, playing shortstop. He comes up to Charlie Brown, takes a look at him standing on his head, quietly takes off his cap and lays it down. Then he puts his head on it and stands upside down with Charlie Brown.

That is communication!

I had a neighbor who discerned that I had a problem. I was upside down. My thinking was all askew. But I thought I was a genius at covering it up. Joan, however, knew my life wasn't what it should or could be. In a sense, she took off her cap and stood on her head with me. I've already told you how she did it. She invited me to my first Christian Women's Club luncheon. I accepted that particular invitation after two years of invitations!

There had been no vital communication between Joan and me until I suddenly changed my mind one day and accepted her invitation. As a result of that one experience, I heard a woman communicate something which enabled me to get rightside up!

Joanie's living next door to us was a miracle in itself. Her husband and she had money down on two homes prior to buying the house which made them our neighbors. Each time they strangely and strongly felt the home was not meant for them. The house next door to us could not be sold for a long time, because it was in a probate court situation. Suddenly, however, this was solved and the home became available. Joan and her husband walked into the house about that time, looked at each other, and knew immediately this was the house God intended for them to buy. Thus we became neighbors.

Joanie herself was not accustomed to witnessing to others. She and her husband were Christians, but it had never been impressed upon her before that she should speak to a neighbor about Christ. God distinctly impressed upon her the need to love me. She didn't hear any audible voice, but she knew God spoke to her, telling her I was miserable and hiding behind a mask. She had heard we survived being struck by lightning. When she first met us and mention was made of this event in our lives, Joan said to us, "God must have some special and wonderful plan for your lives."

My answer to that was, "Yes, we got off lucky." I didn't like to think beyond that about the event. I had no desire to pursue this as a topic of conversation and was annoyed when she would try to bring the conversation back to it. Actually, she was only trying to get me to think about it in depth rather than to shrug it off as a "lucky" occurrence.

I considered myself well-read and a fairly interesting conversationalist. There were much more important topics to discuss, I thought.

Joanie told me later that her concern for Roald and me was her first experience of being burdened for someone else's present and eternal well-being. God gave her a hard case when he burdened her with my welfare as a neighbor. I had set up roadblocks everywhere, and when our conversations took turns that were not to my liking, my quick tongue put an end to her questioning and line of reasoning.

Several times Joan tried to talk to me about God. "You had such a close brush with death, Wilma . . ." I'd cut her short and reply, "Honey, heaven is a big place, and don't you worry, I'll get there." Joan knew I wouldn't—not at that juncture in my life. Later she told me, "Wilma, I was scared for you."

My concepts about heaven were very broad at that point and embraced everyone. It did not matter what you were. I was even open to the concept of reincarnation. I had it all figured out, even though I had never read the Bible. Even though I had had a firsthand experience with death, when thoughts of death and dying crept into my consciousness, I quickly shoved them aside. Death was too bone-chilling a subject.

After being struck by lightning, Roald and I decided we needed to get involved with a church. I picked the church because I liked the pastor's accent. I also liked the fact that we could believe almost anything we wanted. I had always been for the "underdog" and for "causes" where people were downtrodden. We prided ourselves that we were so magnanimous in our thinking in this regard. I even thought after the accident that maybe God had spared our lives so we could go marching in Selma, Alabama!

After the luncheon experience and my encounter with the reality of Jesus Christ, I didn't know how to handle this newfound revelation of God. More and more, however, I was of the conviction I should tell Joanie exactly what had happened. One day when she walked into the house and left something for me to read, as she was going out, the Lord said to me in that inner voice which I had come to recognize, "Now you tell Joanie what you've been wanting to tell her."

I ran out after Joan and called her name. She stopped, turned, and asked, "What is it, Wilma?"

"Oh, I just wanted to thank you again for taking me to that luncheon that day."

She came back, put her hands on my shoulders, and said, "Wilma," and I looked into her lovely eyes, broke down, and cried, "Joanie!"

We melted into each other's arms. It was like a dam breaking for me. It was an unlocking. "Oh Joanie, it meant so much . . . I think something real has happened in my life. . . ."

"I know it has, Wilma," she replied. There was a quiver in her voice, and tears spilled from her eyes.

I was going through a very traumatic time, and no one knew anything about it. I read the many books and magazines Joanie had supplied, and I read the Bible constantly. As I read about sin and the many ways we displease God, I began to see myself, and what I saw was alarming. I could not see any hope for me. I had learned how to use a concordance, and I was looking up verses in the Bible on subjects of great concern to me.

Now I know God allowed me to go through this. I was trying to find an escape hatch. Both Roald and I had been married and divorced and were now remarried. As far as I could see, I was an adulteress. *This is it,* I thought. *I am wiped out. Am I supposed to go back, divorce Roald, and find my first husband and get him to remarry me?*

I knew my first husband had remarried, and that he had two children by this marriage. *What possible good could be accomplished by breaking up that home?* I reasoned. Yet if I was to experience God's forgiveness, wasn't that what I was supposed to do?

There was great unrest and sorrow in my inner spirit. I was unlearned in the things of the Lord, and while the Holy Spirit had been teaching me, now it was time for me to seek help and fellowship with other believers. This was God's way of bringing me out of my secret service Christianity. The old Wilma still surfaced. She was so accustomed to hiding behind a mask, trying to rationalize her way out of things, and working to earn God's favor, that she found it difficult to let go and give God complete control.

No, you do not have to go back and break up your first husband's marriage, the quiet inner voice told me. I would lie beside Roald at night and cry until the bed shook.

I would get up and go down and cry in another room so Roald would not hear me. God allowed me to go through this so I would give Him first place in my heart and life, because up to this time, Roald was still in first place.

God allowed this for a brief period of time, until I came to the end of myself. Unless God is number one in your life, forget about having real peace and joy.

Finally, one day in my thinking, knowing two wrongs would not make a right, and that I could not go back to my first husband, and being unwilling to give up my relationship with Christ, I found myself saying, *Okay, Lord I would rather live alone with my knowledge of You than live with Roald. I choose You.*

The fifth level of our home and the guest room had become my prayer closet, and down I went there, on my knees, sobbing. *God, I will do anything for You; please give me the joy and the peace You promise in Your Word!* A peace descended, and on my knees I fell into a deep, untroubled sleep for the rest of the afternoon. When I awoke later, the peace was still there. I finally was totally God's. I'd always had Him—since the luncheon that day—but He had not had all of me. I was filled with His Spirit, baptized in His love, accepted in the Beloved.

I was able to share this with Joanie, and she immediately felt free to invite me to become part of a Bible study. Until I shared with her what had happened at the luncheon, she had wisely waited.

One day at Bible study, the pastor's wife casually said to me, "Wilma, have you been distressed?"

I was honest with her—indeed, this was a new Wilma—and I replied, "Yes, sort of. . . ."

"Let me give you some verses," she said, and she opened her Bible and read, " 'Therefore if any man be in Christ, he is a new creature: old things are passed away; behold, all things are become new' " (2 Cor. 5:17).

I read the remainder of the verses in that chapter, and tears welled up in my eyes. "For he hath made him to be sin for us, who knew no sin; that we might be made the righteousness of God in him" (v. 21).

Then I looked at Romans 6:6 and knew why I had experienced peace. "Knowing this, that our old man is crucified with him, that the body of sin might be destroyed, that henceforth we should not serve sin." Recognition came that I needed to realize what I had in Christ, and that because of Him, I was dead to sins of the past and alive unto God through His Son. The writings of Paul took on new meaning. "There is therefore now no condemnation to them which are in Christ Jesus, who walk not after the flesh, but after the Spirit" (Rom. 8:1).

CHAPTER 13

A First Fruit

"When I use a word," Humpty Dumpty said to Alice in Wonderland, "I mean just what I choose that word to mean, nothing more, nothing less." I often think about that, and about the direction my life took after I was willing to admit that sin is sin and that all my careful efforts to win God's applause and approval were meaningless. Our will is that which separates us from God, and until we accept Christ, all our good works and efforts to please Him are as filthy rags, even as Isaiah says, "But we are all as an unclean thing, and all our righteousnesses are as filthy rags . . ." (Isa. 64:6).

Many times people have misunderstood my testimony. I do not want that to happen as you read this book. They will say, "Isn't that something; they were struck by lightning, and they found God."

No, we did not. We were struck by lightning and we *did not* find God. That happened ten years later.

Many people think, "No, I am not going to die yet, because I do not even have chest pains. I'll wait until the eleventh hour and hope I do not die at 10:30." If that happens, and if you do not have Jesus Christ in your heart, on the basis of God's eternal Word, then you will be separated from Him for all eternity. And eternity is long.

The thought of being separated from my loved ones for eternity was more than I could bear. Roald's daughter was especially dear to me. We were almost like sisters. Saza began to notice the change in me. "What's with Wilma?" she asked her brothers. She caught me listening to a religious radio program on several occasions; another time she saw me with the open Bible. "Do you suppose she is going through the 'change of life' ?" she asked.

I was forty-two then. She talked to her brothers about this several times. I knew Saza was wondering about me, and I was wondering about her and how best to approach her without alienating her.

"Joanie," I said one day, "how am I going to get my husband to really know Christ? And Saza, I'm so worried about her. I'm frightened for them, Joan. . . ."

I was experiencing the same feelings Joanie had felt for me. Joan understood exactly. "Pray and trust God, Wilma. I'm praying, too. You'll see. Just relax. God will show you what to do."

Saza's birthday was coming up. "Can I give you a Bible, Saza?" I asked. I had purchased an *Amplified Bible* for myself, and it was really helping me.

"Okay," she said, "but I really want the book *Leaves of Gold*."

I ended up getting her both for her birthday on August 4, 1966. Saza immediately started reading *The Amplified Bible*. I'd told her to start reading in John's Gospel. But she wasn't ready to do what I suggested. Instead, she started reading in Matthew.

She was doing this reading all by herself, with no questions or prompting from me. I hoped she was reading but refrained from asking.

She got to Matthew 24 and one day my phone rang. "Wilma, did you know that Christ is coming again?"

I sat on the other end of the phone and thought, *Dear Lord, I am so excited, I can't stand it!* Aloud, I responded, "Oh yes, I found that out, too. . ."

She said, "Did you know it before?"

I answered, "No."

"Isn't it something?" she said, excitement mounting in her voice. "Listen to this," she went on, as she began reading to me over the phone.

"That is so great," I said when she finished.

She ended the conversation then, and I began praying, and oh, did I pray!

One morning Saza called again, and that was not unusual. But she kept calling me all that day, and that was unusual. By late afternoon it was as if the Holy Spirit said to me, *She has something to say to you.* We'd been talking off and on the greater share of the day, but I'd sensed there was something more she wanted to say. Finally I asked, "Saza, do you have something you want to tell me?"

She began to cry. I said, "What is it, honey?"

"I received Jesus five days ago, and I have been trying to get up my nerve to tell you all day. . . ."

Then I began to cry, and I was hanging on to the end of the breakfast bar in our kitchen when Roald came in from his office. "What is it? What is it?" he asked, looking fearful.

"Saza has received Christ," I weakly replied, still in somewhat of a daze.

"Oh," he said, and a blank expression crossed his face. Just as quickly he left the room, and I heard him go upstairs. I turned back to the phone and told Saza, "Your father just left the room in a state of shock, I think." We talked a few moments longer.

I sat there pondering what to do next. I'm not sure just how long it was. Then I heard Roald coming back down the stairs. In a moment he came into the room and put his hands on my shoulders. "Thank you for what you have done for my girl," he quietly said.

A couple of years prior to this Saza had come close to having a nervous breakdown. I had drawn particularly close to her through that experience. But since becoming a Christian, my love and concern for Saza had become evident to Roald and, unknown to me, he had been watching with interest. Now he looked at me and said, "Now I have two of you." I did not get the significance of that statement at the time.

"Oh, honey, isn't this wonderful?" I said. When I looked up at Roald I realized I was crying. I was so excited. Saza was now the second person to receive Christ in our family, and my joy was full to overflowing.

CHAPTER 14

Transformed!

For years I'd been an agile dodger. If someone tried to get near me with Bible verses, or if someone had what I felt was a "holier-than-thou" attitude, I dodged them as often as I could. When I couldn't dodge them, I erected an imaginary wall to put something between them and me. I was a good brick layer, building a wall to defend my position.

I have since come to recognize there are many who go through life doing the same thing. We think we can keep people out of our lives by building these walls as a kind of barrier. I learned, in my wall-building days, that some people knew how to vault right over walls. This made me angry on more than one occasion, and I determined that the next time I was threatened, I would build my wall higher.

Then I found that people liked to tie favorite Bible verses to bricks, and they could throw them over the wall. It was then I really became an agile dodger. But one day I was urged to walk to the end of my wall, come out, and have lunch. Time out! I would have a nice time, see a fashion show, and it would not be too religious—especially since it was being held at my favorite country club. I felt it was safe to take a chance. It just so happened that when the speaker shared that day, I was on the wrong side of the wall. Actually, God brought the wall down!

As I thought about that, reflecting on those many times when I had shut others out of my life by refusing to listen to or accept what they were trying to say or do for me, I realized what they had tried to do. As someone has said, Christian evangelism is nothing but one beggar sharing with another beggar where the bread is. As Christians, we need to expose others to the good news of the gospel. Perhaps we cannot get them to church, but most women, in particular, do enjoy a lovely luncheon.

After Saza shared with me over the phone what had happened to her, I knew I had to invite her to a Christian Women's Club luncheon. She had not erected any walls and was eager to attend.

After the luncheon, we came back to our house. Saza was leaving when Roald drove up. He waved goodbye to her, and as he and I walked in the house, he asked, "How did she like it?"

"She loved it, Roald, just loved it! Honey, I told her what you did when you were a little boy, and she wondered why you had never told her."

"What?" he said.

"Remember what you told me, how you accepted Christ when you were eight and went forward?"

"Oh," he said, looking really distressed, and he walked up the stairs to our bedroom.

I was concerned but decided to leave him alone. I went into the kitchen and started dinner. Several times I stopped, dried my hands, and started toward the door. *No,* that inner voice deep within said. *Let him alone.*

When dinner was ready, I called Roald on the intercom. He came down and I noticed his eyes were a little red. Two weeks earlier, when Saza had called and he'd come home, I'd noticed his eyes were red then, too.

"Wilma, when you put Lisa to bed tonight, after that I want to talk to you."

I couldn't wait to put her to bed. When I came back down, Roald was waiting. "When you said that—after work tonight, when I came home and Saza was leaving—about my inviting Christ into my life as a boy, something broke inside, and I had to be alone. I just went upstairs, got on my knees by the bed and said, 'Christ, if You are not in my heart, I want You to come in right now.' Wilma, it was just like a dam breaking, and I know Christ came into my heart. I haven't cried like this before, but I just broke up. Just as you took Lisa up to bed now, I was sitting here knowing you were coming down, and I was thinking, *This is ridiculous, it was just an emotional experience, you are a man.* But again, the overwhelming feeling of the

Lord came upon me, and I know the Lord said to me, 'Don't ever doubt Me like that again.' "

Again Roald started crying. I put my arms around him, dropped to my knees, and we prayed together. My husband became a totally transformed man. That was October 14, 1966, two weeks after his daughter's encounter with the reality of Christ. By the end of November that same year, my beloved twin stepsons, their wives, and our son-in-law were all born again. It was like dominoes—one falls and they all fall.

CHAPTER 15

Hunger and How to Get Fed

One day my cleaning lady said to me, "What's with your neighbor? I thought you couldn't stand her, and you preferred not to have anything to do with her. Now she's popping in here all the time, and the two of you always have your noses over that book. . . ."

I looked at my cleaning lady and laughed. What she said was true. On numerous occasions I had vented my displeasure at Joanie in the presence of my cleaning lady. I explained, "I love her now. She took me to a luncheon and it was the greatest thing. I have become a Christian. Would you like to go to the next luncheon with me?"

I took her, and she received Christ as we drove home later.

Eight months later—after all this had happened, beginning with my own transformation—Joan asked her pastor, "What am I going to do with these people? Can someone help out with a Bible study or something? These people are all very hungry for the Word."

Pastor Churchill looked at Joanie, smiled,

thought for a moment, and replied, "Why can't I do it?" Thus began Bible studies in our home every Friday night. The pastor fed us like the mother bird does her baby birds, chirping and waiting in the nest. We were just that hungry. This continued for two years without letup.

We left the church we had attended for ten years and became members of Joanie's church. It made a tremendous difference in our lives. I am always quick to tell new believers to get into a Bible-believing church where the pastor really preaches the Word.

Six months after my commitment to Christ, I was asked to share my conversion experience at a church retreat. When I was first asked, I politely refused.

"Just get up and give your testimony," they said.

"No," I said. "I can't do that. . . ."

"Okay, I will pray about it," my neighbor Joanie said. She knew how to handle me. I went home, and sure enough, the Lord began to deal with me.

I called her and said "Okay."

Pants suits were the vogue for women at that time. I went to the retreat with my new pants suit, camel hair with a turtle neck. There was a roaring fire in a big log cabin fireplace, and as I gave my testimony, I was just roasting. By the time I finished, I was drenched in perspiration. I will never forget it. Later I read in Isaiah that God said when we walk through the fire, we will not be burned, and the flames won't consume us. I could look back and regard the moment with some degree of humor. It was a sort of baptism by fire!

I had been a Christian for about two years when I was asked to speak for a Christian Women's Club dinner. It was to be an evening banquet for business women in a small town nearby. Roald and Lisa drove with me. "Don't get up from your knees until I'm all finished," I begged, as I walked out the motel door. By now I had come to realize the effectiveness of intercessory prayer.

I shared that night, but I was not totally honest. I would not take the mask off. I was honest enough about the story and what had happened to us, but I would not reveal what a phony I'd been for so many years. I challenged no one to receive Christ. When I finished I said "Thank you" and sat down.

Immediately God began to speak to my spirit. I was in misery. The only time you are without joy and peace in your Christian walk is when you are bucking something. You will have a rough time until you make peace with God about what He wants you to do and say. I thought, *This will never do. Well, I'll just never do that again.* Much as I enjoyed and appreciated Christian Women's Club, I decided I could not speak for groups such as that.

But God had other plans.

CHAPTER 16

Airborne for the Lord

The call was from Austin, Minnesota. It was an evening Christian Women's Club dinner meeting. Would I come and share? I went through the same feelings of panic. In the end, I consented. It was February, 1969.

"Pray for me on your knees," I told family members and friends.

I had learned my lesson. Or so I thought. I wanted to be obedient to the Lord and honest with the women. I had learned enough to know when you are in the will of God, He will direct you. I had prayed, "Not my will, Lord, but Thine be done." I had confessed my reluctance to accept speaking engagements. "God, I really don't want to go out speaking." I was having a great time underlining books and various versions of the Bible. I was reading, studying, taking courses. But I wasn't particularly eager to go out and share what I was learning.

How do you determine the will of the Lord? Through trial and error I had discovered that when the circumstances of your life, and the Word of God—the Bible—and your inner feelings come together, you can take it as coming from the Lord. The Holy Spirit is telling you something.

I was like Gideon in a sense, Gideon with his fleece, as told in Judges 6:37. After the Austin meeting, I confessed to God I didn't feel I'd done my best again for Him. If it was all right by Him, I'd just as soon not do that again. I boldly stated I'd put out a fleece. If He wanted me to do more speaking, then a call should come in immediately.

I could not imagine that such a call would be forthcoming. But no sooner had I said those words than the phone rang.

Would I come to East Grand Forks, North Dakota?

I felt greatly humbled before the Lord. Unmistakably, God was trying to get a point across to me. He had work for me to do.

I had to get on a plane to keep that engagement. I had not been able to fly for over ten years, you may recall, without fortifying myself with a couple of cocktails before boarding a plane. I was always restless until the stewardess took our orders on the plane.

With no thought or need of cocktails, I got on the plane by myself and flew to East Grand Forks. I spoke before a luncheon gathering and leveled with everyone.

"I am a transformed phony. . . . For years I tried to repay God for sparing my life. I was an expert at playing games. . . ."

That night I spoke for a Christian Business

Women's Council meeting. I cannot forget it. At the two meetings that day, seven women prayed to receive Christ. I was launched. I was airborne for the Lord. From that moment on I had peace and joy and complete freedom in the Holy Spirit. God opened my mouth and filled it.

My red Bible was loaded with verses I had found and claimed. They were written on the flyleaves in the front, so I could read them and fortify myself for speaking for Jesus. I can look in that old Bible today and read these verses:

Come and hear, all ye that fear God, and I will declare what he hath done for my soul (Ps. 66:16).

For I the LORD thy God will hold thy right hand, saying unto thee, Fear not; I will help thee (Isa. 41:13).

And I have put my words in thy mouth, and I have covered thee in the shadow of mine hand . . . (Isa. 51:16).

Be not afraid of their faces: for I am with thee to deliver thee, saith the LORD. Then the LORD put forth his hand, and touched my mouth. And the LORD said unto me, Behold, I have put my words in thy mouth (Jer. 1:8,9).

And he hath put a new song in my mouth, even praise unto our God: many shall see it, and fear, and shall trust in the LORD (Ps. 40:3).

I read these verses over and over on the plane that day on my way to East Grand Forks, and God met me in His Word with strength to obey Him.

103

I started speaking for CWC all over the country. I became actively involved with our local CWC in speaking and teaching Bible studies, and as coordinator for the Friendship Bible Coffees. As a board member for our area CWC, I made many new friends, and my life was greatly enriched by association with these godly women.

Often I heard women say, "If only I had your opportunities. . . ." I learned to respond to that by reminding them God provides opportunities for each of us, wherever we are. Our part is simply to be available and to listen to His leading in our inner being as we devote ourselves to searching the Word.

I took a Campus Crusade "spiritual breathing" evangelism course. Learning these principles helped me immensely.

I discovered that Jesus Christ, at the right hand of God, acts as my Advocate—my Attorney. I made the life-changing discovery that I can call Him up any moment of the day when I have sinned, and He always hears me. His telephone number is 1 John 1:9. "If we confess our sins, he is faithful and just to forgive us our sins, and to cleanse us from all unrighteousness." This means I agree with my Lord, that He is faithful and forgives, and that there is an extra dividend—He cleanses me from *all* unrighteousness. I learned to take my cleansing and then ask the Holy Spirit to fill me and guide me. What freedom! What joy!

It was a thrilling moment for me the day I

discovered Ephesians 6, which speaks of the Christian's armor.

. . . be strong in the Lord, and in the power of his might.

Put on the whole armor of God, that ye may be able to stand against the wiles of the devil . . . Wherefore take unto you the whole armor of God, that ye may be able to withstand in the evil day, and having done all, to stand.

Stand therefore, having your loins girt about with truth, and having on the breastplate of righteousness;

And your feet shod with the preparation of the gospel of peace;

Above all, taking the shield of faith, wherewith ye shall be able to quench all the fiery darts of the wicked.

And take the helmet of salvation, and the sword of the Spirit, which is the word of God (vv. 10–17).

A good soldier does not keep his sword hidden. He keeps it within reach, ready for use. It was a revelation for me to read these grand truths and to make the application personal. This armor is meant to protect us. It was a revelation as I reread and studied these verses to realize there is no provision made for the backside of an individual. I thought about that, then realized why. Christians are to advance, not retreat.

At the time of this writing, I have been sharing what Christ has done in my life for more than ten years. Through these years I have met women in every strata of society—from the top professional to the domestic laborer to the very poor. Without exception, they all have the same need. They need Jesus. Very often, I have discovered, they wear the same mask. There may be little deviations in their masks, but basically they are the same.

CHAPTER 17

Don't Be Fooled
by the Face I Wear

For more years than I care to remember, I wore masks to conceal my real identity. I was an upside down person, to be sure. One day I was looking for something to use when I was to be a World Day of Prayer speaker. I was looking at a *Young Life* magazine, and a poem entitled "Please Hear What I'm Not Saying" seemed to jump out at me. I knew immediately I was to share it. It communicates, better than anything I have ever come across, the kind of person I was for so many years.

I retitled the poem "Masks," and have taken some liberties in changing it to fit me, but it is powerful. Wherever I go, people tell me they identify with it.

Don't be fooled by me.
Don't be fooled by the face I wear,
for I wear a mask, I wear a thousand masks,
masks that I'm afraid to take off,
and none of them are me.

Pretending is an art that is second nature to me,
but don't be fooled,
    please don't be fooled.

Struck by Lightning, Then by Love

I give you the impression that I'm secure
that all is sunny and unruffled with me,
within as well as without,
that confidence is my name
and coolness my game,
that the water's calm and I'm in command,
and that I need no one.
But don't believe me.
Please.

My surface may seem smooth,
    but any surface is a mask,
beneath lies the real me
in confusion, in fear,
    in aloneness, but I hide this.
I don't want anybody to know this,
I panic at the thought of my weakness
    and fear of being exposed.
But I hide this.
That's why I frantically create a mask
    to hide behind.[1]

—Claudia Seiler Brau

I learned the "art" of wearing masks as a child. I
developed the art as I became a young woman. I
never confided in anyone how hurt I was or how
rejected I felt. Not having a mother was a wipeout. But I let no one in my peer group know my
true feelings.

I knew that for years I had engaged in conversation that was nothing more than sustained trivial-
ity. But I knew I was not alone in supporting this

[1]Used by permission of the author.

facade. My speaking took on an urgency prompted by my concern. I discovered many women hovered on the brink of despair. Thoughts of suicide plagued them.

After a newspaper story about me, I received a telephone call. "I am ready to end my life. There is nothing worth living for." I listened as the woman poured out her heart in a story with overtones similar to stories other women had shared with me.

"Listen to me," I said. "There is hope. Everything you read in that newspaper article about me is true. I've been there. I know what you are going through. . . ."

I asked her to meet me for coffee. "No, no," she protested, "I can't do that."

I pleaded with her. "You picked up that phone and called me, and that is the Holy Spirit working in your heart. There are answers. Believe me, there is help and there is hope. I wore masks for years. Take yours off, and come on out and meet me. It will be just you and me."

She finally agreed to meet me at a nearby restaurant. "If I do not show up, don't be too upset," she said, hedging.

"You *will* show up," I replied. "In the meantime, I will be praying." I went to the restaurant and sat and prayed. When the door opened and the woman walked in, I knew it was she, though I had no idea what she looked like. She sat down, and we talked.

Calmly I said, "You need Jesus." I began to explain what He had done in my life and what He meant to me, and what He could mean to her. God was present in that brief encounter. Shirley left that restaurant without her mask. She was transformed by the power of the love of Christ, which had reached and changed her.

Two weeks later I had a luncheon for Vicki, the reporter who had written the newspaper article about me, and for the near-suicide, Shirley. The reporter's life had been changed, too. I remember saying, "Let me tell you what Jesus has done through you, Vicki, and through the story you wrote. In writing that account, God has already used your life in a marvelous way."

I have pictures of the two of them meeting the first time. Today we three are sisters in Christ.

God provided me with many opportunities to witness for Him. Each was a new and refreshing experience.

Within a year of my encounter with the reality of Christ's love, I was asked to teach a college-age class in our church. Then our church started Bible studies, and they grew beyond our imagining. "Hey," we'd say, "we've got something really good going at our house Friday nights—Bible studies. Come and join us."

For many years Roald and I belonged to a bowling league. It was a big thing on Friday nights. We'd bowl, and then everyone would go over to the country club afterward. In the summer months it was golf and then the country club. Our lifestyle revolved around these and other activities with our friends. There is nothing wrong with bowling or golf, but when it came time to sign up for the bowling league, something said, "Don't," and we listened. Friday nights became our time of learning, as we all gathered around the Bible in our home, with Pastor Ken Churchill leading.

While I was on a speaking trip in the South, a friend in Chattanooga, Tennessee, asked, "Wilma, would you like a good definition of communication?" He proceeded to share a discovery he had made.

"Communication is the meeting of meaning between minds." I ran that through a couple of times and had to admit it was *very* good.

Most of us have had the experience of talking to a child, or to anyone for that matter, when we know what we are saying, and we try valiantly to get our point across, but we are met with a look of puzzlement and bewilderment on his or her face. There has been no meeting of meaning between minds.

If you persist in explaining, and if you are fortunate, a light goes on in his eyes, and he says: "Oh, *now* I see what you mean." There has been a meeting of meaning between minds.

Dr. John Drakeford, in his captivating book *The Awesome Power of the Listening Ear*, says communication depends on two things. First there are the physiological aspects of the ear. The mechanism of the ear itself has three parts: the external ear, the middle ear, and the inner ear. Each plays a special role in hearing. Then there is the psychological aspect, where the mind becomes engaged to the ear, and that is called listening. "The brain itself is programmed by years of experience and conditioning to handle the auditory impressions with which it is fed," Drakeford says. It is a selective process. "From the total number of our auditory impressions we choose a small select number upon which to focus our attention. As the sounds come to us we *hear;* when we apply ourselves to their meaning and significance we *listen.* . . . Most humans are engaged in a lifelong process of gradually building up their own personal internal ear plugs and training themselves to ignore certain sounds."[1]

Drakeford gives the illustration of his living in a house located near a railroad track. For the first few nights, every passing train disturbed his sleep. As time went on, he grew less aware of the nearby train activity. One evening a visitor asked if the passing trains bothered him. He replied, "What trains?" His internal "squelching mechanism" had taken over, and he no longer listened to the railroad noises.

I can identify with that. I find that many others can, too. Many of us went as children to Sunday school and church. We heard a lot of God-words

[1]Dr. John Drakeford, *The Awesome Power of the Listening Ear* (Dallas: Word Books, 1967) pp. 18–19.

and a lot of sounds that had no meaning to us. We conveniently tuned them out. We were hearing, but not listening.

Drakeford uses the analogy of an efficient secretary sorting correspondence, keeping only the most important things out for her busy boss's perusal. We do the same thing—we reject some sounds, others have our total attention.

That is what I had done in my life until the luncheon encounter with Christ. I was the big boss. My little internal secretary monitored all incoming conversations, invitations, and anything that might interfere with my lifestyle. Many things got tossed out for being "irrelevant." Life was to be lived, not spent sitting in Sunday school or church listening to things that had no meaning, as I'd had to do as a child. So the masks went up as I went about this business of living. But inwardly I was crying, *Don't be fooled by the face I wear.*

CHAPTER 18

Focus in Crisis

I saw a cartoon which confirms my oft-expressed belief that some days you just don't know which end is up. Things can become confusing.

The cartoonist depicts a worm crawling through the grass. The sun is smiling down, and it is a lovely day. The worm, a smile on his face, is peering back at what appears to be another worm. The worm admits that springlike days compel worms like him to lose their sense of reason. He's love-struck! The object of his love appears lovely, so lovely in fact he asks the other worm to marry him. The worm's response is "Go roll your loop, my looney friend, I happen to be your other end."

Often we take the binoculars of our mind and look through the wrong end, viewing the problems of our life and distorting them instead of magnifying the Lord. How do you magnify the Lord? He is already Lord and cannot be enlarged upon. He is already everything, but what we need to do is enlarge our vision of Him. If we point the binoculars in the right direction and see Jesus for what and who He is, then we are magnifying Him and diminishing our problems. Too often we magnify the problem.

We had a hole in the liner of our swimming pool. It was close to the surface, so Roald drained some of the water off. I could see the hole, and I took the binoculars, because I am near-sighted, and peered out of the patio doors to examine the hole. All of a sudden, as I held the binoculars up to my eyes, the hole loomed large. It was unpatchable. There was no help for the hole. I went running through the house to find Roald and said, "The hole is too big. It can't be patched."

He came running back with me, looked at the hole, and said, "It's the same size as when we first discovered it."

"No, it isn't," I insisted. But Roald said, "Put the binoculars down, Wilma, and look at the hole. The binoculars are distorting it for you." I felt sheepish as I realized the logic of his statement. Together we walked outdoors and examined the hole. It was small and patchable.

It was a lesson for me. The verse "Don't worry about anything; instead, pray about everything; tell God your needs and don't forget to thank him for his answers" (Phil. 4:6, TLB) came into focus. How easy it is to spout off Bible verses without thinking of their full meaning.

God was going to give us opportunity to put that verse into practice. My husband's multimillion-dollar business was knocked out from under him in one day. What do you do in a situation like that? God assures us in the Bible that if we glorify Him and hold Him up, He will be our strong support. The year 1978 was the most devastating year of our lives, but it was also the most joyous and peace-filled year Roald and I have experienced. That needs explaining.

For years we were accustomed to buying, getting, and giving exactly as we pleased, with little thought to the question that hounds many couples: Can we afford it? Suddenly, with all our income cut, it was a new situation. It may sound simplistic to some, but I know of no other way to say it: At the moment of crisis, God can be depended on.

Prior to such an experience, you sometimes wonder what you would do in just such a circumstance. Whenever I had such a thought I quickly dismissed it—it's a pretty scary thought to entertain. You think you could not weather such a storm. But when that time comes, on the basis of our experience, I can tell you that God is right there.

To fully understand what happened to us, you should know that within a year after we became Christians, my husband called a meeting of the shareholders of the business. This included his sons (the twins), his daughter, and her husband. Roald announced the company was being turned over to the Lord. Roald had read some books by Christian businessmen, and the book *God Owns My Business*, by Stanley Tam, impressed him.

The executives of the company were at this meeting. Roald said he did not like some of the things that were common business practices and said his salesmen would not do these any longer. One of the first things he did was to call in the "Playboy Club" keys.

One of the vice-presidents of the company became very upset and accused Roald of losing his mind. He announced that he differed with Roald's views and objectives. In the next several years this man set out to ruin my husband and the business. The first thing we lost were the "Playboy" accounts—the accounts we previously had entertained lavishly. This man also took some of the formulas Roald had developed. The company started going down.

In our Bible studies, Roald shared what was happening. "But we are just going to continue to trust God," he announced.

We were involved in supporting missionary programs, kids in Campus Crusade, and many religious radio and television ministries, in addition to our own church. Before Christ entered our lives (B. C. days, I call them), when the stewards of the church came around to ask us to raise our pledge, I would caution Roald against giving too much. After our lives were transformed, this kind of attitude changed completely, and we found great joy and satisfaction in giving. We knew we could never outgive God.

When the business started going downhill,

Roald said, "I think this is what is called 'testing.' We will just hang in there, and if no one says anything about the man who has done this to us, everything will work out. Let's just pray and continue to trust God." Roald was like a rock as he led all of us, and we willingly followed his lead.

Within a year God reversed the bad situation. We got many of the accounts back. Companies who learned our business was Christ-centered started doing business with us. We began one of the most prosperous times in our lives. We became Christians in 1966, and by early 1968 business was rolling in. We became known internationally as a Christian business organization you could trust.

We prospered financially, but the greater prosperity was our spiritual welfare. The witness of Roald, his sons, Ron and Rollie, and our son-in-law, Bud, brought many men into a relationship with Christ.

In 1975 an eastern syndicate bought out our competition, forming what is called a conglomerate. They went after all the business in the field. We continued to pray and trust God. There are those who imply by their testimonies that when you become a Christian everything comes up roses, and you will not have problems or temptations. That's not an altogether accurate portrayal.

I want to be a witness in stating I have complete victory in the midst of *not* knowing what is going to happen next.

We kept praying and thought, *Surely God will not let this happen to us. We won't lose our business; we've worked too hard for this, and we've been honest.* We trusted and our faith did not waver. There was no moaning by any of our family team. "We know this is Your business, Lord, and whatever happens is according to Your plan. . . ."

Things continued to get tighter. In 1977 our competition lost sixteen million dollars fighting us and it didn't even affect them, they were so big. For us it was the beginning of the wipeout. We lost between a half and one million dollars. We were slowly going down but still trusting, believing God was going to do some miraculous thing to pull us out.

At the end of October, 1977, Roald and I left town and headed for Florida. I was on a speaking schedule that would take us down the east coast of Florida. We arrived in Florida at our condominium and the phone rang. The twins told us what we had been expecting, although we had been reluctant to articulate it even to each other. The boys broke the news that we'd been forced into Chapter Ten, bankruptcy.

The boys immediately countered with Chapter Eleven, voluntary bankruptcy. As Christians, we felt we should pay our bills—this was our witness and the thing to do.

We thought, *God, how can You let this happen to us? We are Christians, and this is bad, to owe money. Vindicate Your name, God, pull us out.*

One moment we were feeling that way, the next we were praising Him and trusting. The courts stepped in and began to monitor everything. Then they began to cut personnel and expenses to the bone. The first head to roll was my husband's—the founder and chairman of the board. As of December 1, 1977, we were totally without income. If my husband has any outstanding gift, it is the gift of giving. This was a tremendous shock to us, and one of the things that made us feel especially bad was to know our giving would suffer.

I was to begin speaking on November 3. The first thing that happened, after receiving the distressing news at Sanibel Island, Florida, was that I had a "pity party." I am not a super-saint. Roald and I reacted in a very human way. Like David, the psalmist, we cried out, "Oh God!"

We both went into a mild state of shock. I could not fully comprehend what was happening. I kept my speaking engagement, but I felt numb. As the shock passed, I began to get the full impact. The first few days, my husband and I seemed to take turns—first he was down and I was up, then it reversed. I would weep and he would say, "Wilma, we must trust the Lord; He knows all about it."

It was amazing the way we were able to minister to each other.

The shock was tempered by God's grace and mercy. We were able to bear it. But there is something about the first and the fifteenth of the month, when you are accustomed to a check coming in, that suddenly reminds you—the fifteenth will be no different than the first! There would be a moment of shaking and quaking in the spirit before turning it over to God.

Through it all, on that busy preplanned speaking trip, I didn't miss a single speaking engagement, and I was booked heavily. I found myself —without prearrangement or forethought— reaching a point in my sharing where I would say, "Let me tell you what kind of God I have—I have joy and peace, but I have problems, too." I then would tell them frankly about my husband's business. "One day you own a multimillion-dollar business; the next day it is totally knocked out, and you expected God to intervene all along. What do you do?"

I cannot describe the joy that flooded me each time I began to share in this way. God was faithful. I believe we are in training here for reigning there. This thought captured my attention when I read God has to raise us, His children, and prepare us for our heritage. If you give a child everything he wants, what happens? The child becomes bored, dissatisfied, and many times worthless to himself and society. You have given him everything he wants, and he is looking not at you, but at what you can give him and what he wants. You have lost your position. When you say no to the child—and he begins to work and earn money to get what he needs and wants and to go through a little suffering—then the character of that child has an opportunity to develop.

God is developing our character here on Earth so we can be what He intends us to be in heaven. I find this concept exciting. We go through disappointments, harassments, misunderstanding, and criticism. These can be either stumbling stones or stepping stones. You can either react according to the way God's Word teaches you, or you can react contrary to His Word. If you examine your reaction, you will know if it is right.

Out of this experience God has allowed us to witness of our confidence in *Him* and His all-knowing wisdom to many people in all walks of life. One of these men was Dave Parr, who had been a top Washington lobbyist for many of the large milk companies in the United States. We flew him into Minneapolis in an advisory capacity to consult with us on our business. The outcome of this meeting was that instead of hearing much about our business problems, he heard about Jesus. Dave said he'd been searching all his life for something to *really* give his life to—something with ultimate meaning. Dave turned his life over to the Lord and is today serving God.

The grace of God is there for each of us, whether we know it or not. God has promised to be with us. He cares for us. I shall never forget a story I heard which beautifully demonstrates this. A man died and went to heaven, and God said to him, "I am going to review your life for you. There are some things I want you to see." Passing in review was the man's whole life—all the mountain peak experiences, the times when he was really up and when life was so good. But he also saw the valleys, and how down he became—all those experiences were there, too.

The man noticed there were always two sets of footprints in every mountain experience, but in the valley experiences he saw only one set of footprints. He said, "Jesus, tell me why when things were going so great You were always there with me, but when things were so bad, You left me to walk alone?"

Jesus lovingly looked at the man and replied, "Those are not your footprints, they are Mine. I was carrying you."

That is the point—He carries us. Make yourself conscious of the fact that at *all* times, Jesus is there with you.

CHAPTER 19

Breaking Bad Habits

Once God has begun a good work in you, He continues it. If becoming a Christian depended on perfection, then I would never have made it. I had some bad habits (and still do), but there were things in my life I was reluctant to part with. When the parting finally came, it was painful in many respects.

I've often thanked God that perfection is not the criterion by which He judges us. Having said that, however, let me hasten to add that I know the Bible says, "Be ye therefore perfect, even as your Fatner wnich is in heaven is perfect" (Matt. 5:48). That verse troubled me until I studied it in *The Amplified Bible*. There it is explained. "You, therefore, must be perfect, as your heavenly Father is perfect (that is, grow into complete maturity of godliness in mind and character, having reached the proper height of virtue and integrity)."

Life is a growing process. In this never-ending process, as I first began growing in ways I knew would be pleasing to God, I recognized I had bad habits that needed breaking.

It was as though I were in a rowboat with the Lord at the oars. He said, "Wilma, put your other foot in the boat, we are going into deep water, and you will like it." But I had, as it were, one foot on shore and one in the boat.

"No," I was in effect saying to Him, "I have to get back to our friends and our lifestyle. I can't let Roald know what has happened, it might ruin our marriage. . . ." I was afraid the Christian life would be detrimental to our way of life. How wrong I was! As I began to grow, I began to see that Christ enhanced our lives. He did not spoil, take away enjoyment, or detract from our life-goals in any way.

It was as if I were doing the splits, however, and had it not been for the grace of God and His power in my life, I would never have made it. He, through His indescribable love and mercy, got me to swing that other leg into the boat. But it didn't happen overnight.

The God who made us knows how to handle us. We are His creation, unique and, as Donna Axum, former Miss America and now a radiant Christian, says, "We are Designer originals." I began to come under conviction about certain areas and habits in my life as God spoke to me through His Word. Neglect of the Bible causes stunted Christians. Growth comes as we nurture the inner man by reading and applying the Word of God.

Before my encounter with Christ I mistakenly thought Christianity was a set of rigid do's and don'ts. God knew I was looking for an escape hatch, and if I met one Christian who said to me, "You aren't supposed to do that . . . ," I would have found it. But no such escape hatch in the form of uptight Christians came my way.

I had troubled thoughts about smoking. These thoughts started after about six months of being a Christian. I found myself thinking, *Wilma, you have received Christ into your life, isn't it about time you gave up smoking?* Then I would excuse myself by reminding the Lord and myself, *Look, I've been smoking twenty-two years, I'm not about to quit now. It's a habit, and lots of people have habits a lot more offensive than smoking.* I would go to Christian Women's Club luncheons and smoke furiously. There were ashtrays on the tables, and I felt comfortable with my habit. My neighbor Joan never said a word, though I kept waiting for her to pounce on me.

Joan frequently came over. It seemed every time she'd swing open the top of the dutch doors and say "Good morning," I'd be snubbing out my cigarette. One day, with a trace of irritation, I said, "Joanie, do you always have to come over right about the time I'm lighting a cigarette?"

"Go ahead," she replied. "When have I ever said anything to you about your smoking habit?" That took care of the subject with Joan in short order.

One day, which I can only attribute to the power of the Holy Spirit, I didn't like the smell of my undergarments. They smelled like smoke! I then sniffed at some of my other clothes. *Smoke!* I used the finest colognes, deodorants, and bath products on the market. *This is strange*, I thought. *It's never bothered me before.* Then I recalled that Lisa, our little girl, had been asking me for a couple years, "Mama, why do you smoke?" That was getting to me, and now it really got to me. *God,* I asked, *are You trying to tell me something?* Deep inside, in that inner voice I had come to recognize, God questioned me. *Would you like it taken away, Wilma?*

The first attempt to stop smoking came after my stepdaughter received Christ. I knew God had forgiven me for my first failed marriage, for my divorce, and my remarriage, but it was hard to forgive myself. As I studied the Bible and as we had our Bible study classes, I learned about the enemy's tactics. Still I carried a heavy burden of guilt. Then when Saza received Christ, I was *so* happy. Early one morning I awakened with the thought that if God could use me as an instrument in Saza's awakening, then surely God had forgiven me. With that knowledge I was able to finally forgive myself.

I went downstairs early that morning, saying, "Oh thank You, Jesus, thank You, thank You. What can I do for You?" No sooner had I said that than I realized what I could do.

"I'll give You my cigarettes right now," I said. I looked at my watch. It was 4 A.M., and as I was thanking the Lord, I was smoking. I put the cigarette out and thought, *There God, I have paid*

You back. The old habit patterns of trying to pay God back were still deeply ingrained.

I went back to bed. Upon awakening a few hours later, my first thought was, *Oh, what did I do earlier this morning!*

The next thought was, *Don't tell Roald, because you might slip.* How sneaky the enemy is!

Then the inner voice said, *Get up and tell your husband what you told Me you would do.*

I talked to Roald while he was shaving and said, "I want you to know that at 4 A.M. I gave up my cigarettes."

"That's great," he replied. "Why don't you tell Lisa?" Our bedroom was on the fifth level; six or seven steps down was Lisa's bedroom. I just called out, "Lisa, come up here, I want to talk to you."

She came up and I dramatically said, "You will never see your mother smoke again. *Never!*"

She was still half asleep, and so she groggily answered as she looked up at me, "Okay, that's neat, Mom," and made her way back down the steps. That was that. Lisa never did *see* me smoke again, but I'm sorry to have to tell you I did smoke again.

I now tell people who are trying to change their bad habits in such dramatic ways to let God take care of those things in their lives. Give Him the right to change you; tell Him you are willing to give up bad habits and to change, then cooperate with Him by doing the things you know you should do.

Recognize that sometimes it takes time. Actually I went through a ridiculous period of time.

I made my husband quit smoking because I found in the Bible that we can be stumbling blocks to others. I told him he was a stumbling block with his smoking. Roald quit for my sake, and it was no big deal with him. But I was still left with the habit.

It was funny in some respects, as I look back on it now. I would cheat. I would run up to what was a carriage house on our property that we had converted into a garage. I would jump in my car and drive two miles to the nearby village for a pack of cigarettes.

As time went on and I was becoming better known in the area as a Christian and was going to a local Bible college, I felt embarrassed to go into the drugstore to buy cigarettes. I finally ran out of stores in our vicinity where I could conveniently buy cigarettes to support my habit. We were too well known locally.

I almost ruined the plumbing at our house. I would light a cigarette and then, because I didn't want Roald or my little girl to know it and find the stub, I'd flush it down the toilet. I wasn't enjoying the cigarettes, yet I couldn't give them up. I didn't want anyone to find them, so I began flushing almost entire packages down the drain. The enemy got to me. *Face it, you are wasting money. You know you aren't going to give up smoking, but you can find places to hide them. So just take your carton of cigarettes and put them away.* I then began to hide them under my cashmere sweaters. Before I had smoked half a pack a day. Now I was smoking a whole pack. It was ridiculous. Then I had to cope with the remorse. This conduct continued for almost ten months after that 4 A.M. decision to give up cigarettes "for the Lord." Then one day I said, *Lord, make me sick, anything, but take the habit away.* I became very ill. During seven or eight weeks of that summer I was very sick. There was something wrong with my throat, though there had never been anything wrong with it before. The doctor asked, "How much do you smoke?" I said, "I don't," and he asked, "How much do you cheat?"

I looked at the doctor and wanted to "punch out his lights." I answered, "I smoke very little."

He looked at me and firmly replied, "You are all through cheating."

The doctor ordered me to bed and told me not to talk. That was very difficult. The doctor threatened hospitalization. I then became a more submissive patient.

That summer I studied much and learned a great deal. One day, God said, *You have been learning a lot about Me. When are you going to share?*

In my reading and studying, many times I would think, *Write this down, Wilma, you are going to need it someday.* I formed the habit of keeping notes. At the time I considered it a strange thought. After all these years, as I do more speaking and teaching in seminars, I know why God motivated me to take notes.

That day, as I felt the Lord talking to me, I answered back. *You know, God, I think I could teach a class of fifth or sixth grade girls at Sunday school, if they could use me after I get better.*

At this time Joan came over and asked if Roald and I would consider being advisors for the young people's group at our church. I gave the excuse that Roald wasn't ready yet. How easy it is to speak good thoughts to the Lord; how quick we are to excuse ourselves when opportunities arise!

Within a day or two the telephone rang. It was Bill Perry, a businessman from our church. He said he needed an associate teacher. "I could have called a number of others, Mrs. Stanchfield, but your name kept coming to mind. I'm really quite sure this is of the Lord," he said.

"Well, Mr. Perry," I said, "I've been sick."

"Have you been ill?" he asked surprised.

"It's been close to seven weeks already," I replied.

There was a long pause, then he said quietly, "I really thought the Lord wanted me to call you; now you tell me this. But I am going to go ahead and say this to you—if the Lord is in it, it will come about, and you will be the associate teacher for the college-age class."

The tingle within turned to an icy cold chill. Shocked, I replied, "Oh, I just don't think I could

131

do that." This was in the height of the rebellion on college campuses in the sixties. The very thought of trying to teach college kids was just overwhelming.

"I want you to promise you will think and pray about this. It may very well be of God," he said.

One day he visited me, and we continued our conversation. Mr. Perry shared how he had come to accept Christ, how he was a reformed alcoholic and had once contemplated suicide.

I decided to tell him how God had just taken cigarettes away from me. I had no desire to smoke. He said, "That is good," and shared that he, too, had once had the cigarette habit. He said that even while we'd been talking he had had a tremendous desire to light up a cigarette. I commented, "Oh, I'm so sorry. I didn't mean to disturb you."

"That is alright. You are going to have the desire again, too. . . ." he answered.

"Oh, no," I quickly countered. "God has taken care of that."

"Well if you ever do," he said, "let me tell you how I overcome it. I recognize that it is only a momentary temptation, and I have to be involved in that decision for one split second. I simply say yes to God, and no to the enemy. In that moment, I say, 'God, You take over.' "

We ended our conversation that day, and I promised to commit the need and the request to the Lord and to wait on Him for a sure answer.

One week later I was back on my feet, with the doctor's permission. I had weathered the crisis and was pronounced in good health. I was in the kitchen preparing dinner. I stopped to dry my hands, as was my familiar custom, and reached for my pack of cigarettes. I stopped and remembered what Bill Perry had said. "If you ever are tempted . ." I stood there and thought, *Oh Lord, if Bill Perry could do it, so can I. God, I am saying yes to You and no to the devil.*

There were a couple times after that when I would do battle in this manner with the enemy. I learned at such times to repeat 1 John 1:9: "If we confess our sins, he is faithful and just to forgive us our sins, and to cleanse us from all unrighteousness." I would say ". . . greater is he that is in you, than he that is in the world" (1 John 4:4).

I do not equate dropping bad habits such as smoking with what it means to be a Christian. As I said at the outset of this chapter, if perfection were required, I would have failed at the outset. I would *still* fail, daily. I have had many bad habits to break and many things in my life to contend with that I recognized as not being things which would help me grow toward the maturity of godliness in mind and character the Bible speaks of. Long-entrenched habits of anger and unforgiveness are devastating before the Lord. Our bodies are temples of the Holy Spirit. This includes our mind and emotions. This is plainly taught in 1 Corinthians 3:16, 17, and also in Romans 12:2.

Our bodies are likened to the Old Testament temple. God was zealous about His temple and often reprimanded His people for neglecting it. God's temple, our bodies, is to be respected.

Just as it is with our bodies, so it is with our mind and emotions. We are to honor and respect these physical temples the Creator has given to us. We are to show a single-minded purpose of faithfulness to Christ in "temple" care.

I came to recognize that cigarettes were coming before God. With that recognition came release from the bondage to this bad habit. With it also came the bonus God gives when we obey Him— better health and a good conscience knowing that I honor Him in this regard also.

And oh yes, I did begin work with the college-age class. God had been preparing me for it.

Out of all this came a serious conviction that Christianity certainly isn't merely having the strength to break these physical habits. Rather, it is dealing with the inner man, a cleansing of the inner temple instead of whitewashing the outside. My deceit in trying to hide my habit was uglier in God's sight than the cigarette habit itself. My deeply ingrained habits of anger, pride, retaliation, and deceit were much more a stench in God's nostrils. Many people think that since they don't smoke, or they don't do this or that, this makes them acceptable in God's sight. God looks at the heart. There is where He seeks to see us experience transformation. This is what conforms us to the likeness of His Son.

CHAPTER 20

Satanic Opposition

In the same way that I have learned to say yes to God and no to temptation, I have learned to say no to depression and other satanic attacks. Every day we live we have a choice in the circumstances that confront us. We can react in ways that enable us to grow and bring glory to the Lord, or we can succumb to the vicious opposition of the enemy.

Through the years, as I have gone from place to place sharing what God has done for us, I have known that which I recognize as God's refining process. The Lord allows events to happen. The prophet Isaiah expressed it so well. "For my name's sake will I defer mine anger, and for my praise will I refrain for thee, that I cut thee not off. Behold, I have refined thee, but not with silver; I have chosen thee in the furnace of affliction. For mine own sake, even for mine own sake, will I do it: for how should my name be polluted? and I will not give my glory unto another" (Isa. 48:9–11).

God tells us that if we were to be completely destroyed through that which comes at us with such potent force, then there would not be those left to bring glory to Him. It is an awesome privilege *and* responsibility to be one of God's chosen ones. That is the right of every believer.

When you follow Christ, you can expect opposition. But how easily we forget and begin to wonder why and to complain.

In 1973 Roald and I visited his cousin in Clearwater, Florida. His cousin remarked on how I loved seashells and the ocean. "You really should take her to Sanibel Island, Roald," he said. We thought that was nice but didn't pay much attention to the suggestion. The third time he said it, I asked, "Where is this place?" When we learned it was only 125 miles away, Roald and I looked at each other and said "Let's go!" We went, and I was immediately enchanted by the island. After that visit, we couldn't get the island off our minds.

The next year, Roald asked where I wanted to go for a vacation. I said, "Sanibel Island." Through a remarkable series of events we ended up buying a condominium on the island at a ridiculously low price (in contrast to what they are now selling for).

We met Bart, an interior decorator, and in the process of getting acquainted we learned his wife was suffering from Hodgkin's disease. Instead of discussing our decorating needs, we ended up talking to him about the Lord. We called our Minnesota Bible study group and got the prayer chain started (it goes throughout the country) for Bart's wife Billie. We all prayed for her healing. Then Roald and I shared with Bart what God had done for us and what He could do for him. When we asked Bart if he would like to receive Christ into his life, he cried. When he had regained his composure he asked, "How does it feel to see a fifty-two-year-old man cry like this and to hear his sobs?"

We told him it sounded great. "Those are tears of repentance, Bart. God has begun a good work in you."

"You sound like Anita Bryant," Bart said. "And you remind me of another person, Dale Evans Rogers." I look back on that conversation now and marvel at the way God works. I thank Him also for the outspoken witness of women like Anita and Dale. They will never know on this side of heaven what effect their courageous testimony has had.

When Bart left, Roald and I headed for a Christian bookstore. Bart was taking his wife to Houston for cancer therapy and another examination to see the extent of the disease. I had heard Bart say that at one time they'd been Methodist. I also remembered that Dr. Charles Allen was pastor of a large Methodist church in Houston. At the bookstore we bought Dr. Allen's book on the Twenty-third Psalm. (We had told Bart our experience and what that Psalm meant to us.) We also picked up books by Dale and Anita.

The next day, Roald and I went to the furniture store where Bart worked. When we got there Roald said, "I am going to give him my cross tie-pin." As we walked in, Bart came over and said, "My friends!" We embraced warmly.

"We've gotten a few books for your wife, and

I've written her a note," I said, handing him the books. Then Roald said, "And I want you to have my cross." He removed it and helped Bart put it on.

When Bart and his wife returned from Houston they called and asked us to meet them. Bart had not told us his wife was a Christian and had been praying for him for years. Doctors at the hospital in Houston had not been able to find any symptoms of the disease, and they were mystified. We all knew God had answered our prayer.

That was just the beginning of many wonderful things that happened on Sanibel Island. It is an unfinished story, for we still go back there every opportunity we get.

I was overjoyed when I was asked to lead a Bible study on Sanibel Island. Soon we were able to begin a Christian Women's Club (CWC). Women came to the Bible studies, and there were decisions for Christ. How we praised God!

At our first CWC luncheon, two hundred and fifty women came, and another fifty were turned away. It has been that way ever since it started. Many of the women who came to the Bible studies were later asked to serve on the CWC board, and this was gratifying to me. God put us on that island for several reasons, of that we are convinced. When God is leading you and the light is green, you do not stop at the light and say, "I wonder if I should go." You just move on through. When God says stop, you will see a red light. We felt we had a

green light all the way as we bought the condominium and spent as much time on the island as
we could. Now, as we face the greatest financial
crisis in our lives, we know the investment in that
Sanibel Island home may well be what God uses to
help us get back on our feet in the years ahead. It
was with some pain that we put it on the market.
But the whole purpose of our being there was to be
ambassadors for Him, an extension of His arm.

One of our neighbors on the island is Darlene
Swanson. When a salesman told us, "Your neighbor talks like you do," I knew he meant she, too,
was a Christian. When he told me her name, I
instantly recognized it. "Oh, I know about her," I
exclaimed with delight. "Her story is told in one of
my favorite books, *Cameos, Women Fashioned by
God.*" Darlene and I became close sisters in the
Lord, as well as neighbors. My husband and I felt
our cup of blessing was running over.

In late 1978, as I began to work on this book, we
experienced opposition from the enemy that was
meant, we felt, to keep the story from being told.

I returned from Toronto, Canada, after an ex-
tended speaking trip, and immediately went out
on another speaking trip about seventy-five miles
from Minneapolis. While there I experienced a
recurrence of a bladder infection. My hostess
called our druggist in Minneapolis and asked him
to phone in a prescription to the town where I was
speaking that day and the next. I took one of the
pills and went to bed. A friend, Elaine Gabriel,

was with me. Around four in the morning I woke up feeling very ill. I got up and made my way to the bathroom. When I looked at myself in the mirror I could not believe my eyes.

I was having a violent drug reaction. My lips were swollen so badly that my upper lip was up to my nose, and my bottom lip was equally bad. The lips were so swollen that they were tight against my teeth and affected my speech. (I was to speak at noon that day.) I was covered with a rash like measles all over my arms and legs, and I shook uncontrollably.

I got back into bed, and Elaine knelt by the bed. She prayed and asked God to make it possible for me to keep my speaking commitment. We switched off the lights and left the matter in God's hands. "We trust You, Lord," I said, as I lay there in great misery.

We got an emergency appointment with a doctor for late afternoon. I did speak that noon. My lips were still swollen, but I was able to talk better than I had at four in the morning. Many prayed to receive Christ into their lives.

The moment I finished speaking, Elaine drove us home to Minneapolis. Roald had gotten an appointment with our family doctor, who took me right in. The doctor said it was a miracle I even survived. It was an extreme toxic reaction to sulfa drugs. That type of reaction could have proven fatal. I praise God for my friend, Elaine, who knelt by my bed and prayed.

But then I was immediately attacked again. A friend who had a virus came to visit. Roald was the first one to come down with it. I was busy keeping speaking engagements seminars which I conduct, but within a few days I picked up the virus from Roald, and it went into a bad stage. Among other things I had laryngitis.

In four days I had spoken ten times. The calendar was marked full for the days ahead, but I was unable to speak. We were greatly concerned. In addition, I was experiencing sciatic nerve back pain and could hardly get out of bed. We were scheduled to leave for Florida, where I would be kept busy with CWC luncheon speaking engagements. We were also going to do television taping en route. And we had set aside three days to spend in Nashville to work on this book.

At any point I could have said, "This is it, I cannot take this another moment." I had migraine headaches and wanted nothing more than to just disappear for a while.

At such moments I need to remind myself not to project myself into the next day, or even to the next hour, and certainly not into the next week. The Christian walk is a moment-by-moment, step-by-step adventure in living. It is easy to forget God orders our steps as well as our stops. Life is not to be lived as though it were a marathon race. Proverbs 3 was written by a wise man. "Trust in the LORD with all thine heart; and lean not unto thine own understanding. In all thy ways

acknowledge him, and he shall direct thy paths"
(vv. 5, 6).

David the psalmist wrote for good reason that
"The steps of a good man are ordered by the LORD:
and he delighteth in his way. Though he fall, he
shall not be utterly cast down: for the LORD uphol-
deth him with his hand" (Ps. 37:23, 24).

We kept our appointments and made our way to
Sanibel Island. There were thirteen luncheons
and appointments on the agenda, and the enemy
was not about to leave me alone.

I awoke early one morning with a stabbing pain
in my jaw that kept me awake until daybreak. It
was a rainy and dreary day. Roald called a local
dentist and was able to get me in on an emergency
appointment. "I can't play tennis in the rain," he
quipped to my husband. "Bring her in; we'll take
care of the problem." It was an abcessed tooth.
Four and a half hours in the dental chair and two
hundred dollars later I was back at our condominium. That night, in spite of the root canal
work done earlier in the day, I was able to speak to
a group of business executives. We thanked God
for the rain and for His timing, which enabled
Roald to get the help I needed.

That night I was struck with a virus. Again I
was up most of the night. I felt miserable and
knew it was an intestinal flu. Early in the morning
the devil tried to get to me. "You will never make
it across Alligator Alley, Wilma. That is a long
drive, almost to the east coast of Florida, and
there are no rest-stops in between."

I began praying. "God, You know I need to keep that luncheon appointment. I praise and thank You that You are going to enable me to go." Then I called the devil a liar and said, "It will do you no good to oppose me, for I am going. In Jesus' name I rebuke you, Satan." The act of praising God lifted my spirits. Roald and I started the long drive early in the morning so we could make it by noon. It turned out to be a fabulous day in the Lord. Not only were there great spiritual victories, but the women showered us with financial blessings far above the usual honorarium.

Decentralization is a marvelous modern word that describes the dispersion or distribution of functions and powers from a central authority to regional and local authorities. I find it necessary to decentralize self from the throne and establish Christ as Lord of my life. The way I do this is to say, "Jesus, right now I give my pain and problems to You. You take care of them. I am going to go on about Your business." I find that to be decentralization. He takes over, and I do not have to relate my problems to someone else. I can minister to others or listen to their problems while the Lord is taking care of me.

Satanic opposition comes to me often in the early hours of the day. That can be a low ebb. It is easy to fluctuate in your feelings. One's emotions can be very unstable at 3 or 4 A. M. When you find yourself in this state, you have got to whip out the Sword, the Word of God. It has to be wielded. You have to stand on the Word of God and say "I can do all things through Christ which strengtheneth me" (Phil. 4:13).

One's will is involved at such moments. When I was physically struck on Sanibel Island, my *feelings* were "Don't try to go, don't try to keep those appointments, Wilma." My *mental powers* said, "Use your common sense. You are not well." But with a determination of the *will*, I committed it to God. Later we saw why I had been so viciously attacked. I proved God that day, as I have many times in the past, and He is always faithful. Satan will do everything to defeat us and keep us from doing the Lord's work.

I have also discovered that when the enemy can't defeat me, he will try to get at me through those I love or am associated with in some way. This was demonstrated on a return trip from Sanibel Island to Minneapolis. Once again we stopped off at Nashville to work on this book. My coauthor and I had gotten a good start on working together when it was time to take a break. We left the office building, and as we walked to the car, Helen took a terrible tumble on a slippery incline. She fell spread eagle on the blacktop of the parking lot. Her briefcase skidded across the lot. As she fell I screamed, "Oh no!"

I was certain her entire face would be a bloody mess and that her teeth would be knocked out. It should have incapacitated her. She got up with only two skinned knees and a mark on one hand. "I fell on an angel" were her first words. We both believe this to be true. She was wearing a mauve-colored suede suit—a lovely light color. There was not so much as one spot on the suit, nor was the briefcase scratched or damaged in any fashion.

As we got in the car we thanked God for guardian angels. And I pleaded Christ's blood over Helen so she would not experience any internal injuries or muscle-wrenching discomfort later. We had work to do on this book, and our time together was short. We both felt the enemy would do what he could to keep this book from being written on schedule.

No sooner was that episode behind us, than we encountered still another satanic attack. Roald called Minneapolis to check on our seventeen-year-old daughter. My friend Elaine stays with her when we are gone. Elaine hesitated to tell us, yet knew she had to, that a man's large footprints had been found in the snow under the windows in our daughter's bedroom. Not only that, but Elaine had seen the man lurking behind nearby buildings. We were nine hundred miles from home. All we could do was say, "Father, this is Your department. We need Your help to protect Lisa and Elaine."

If you want to live a *mediocre life*, just pull in, sit back, and do nothing for Jesus. We are in this thing together with Him. He encountered satanic opposition on Earth, so why should we expect anything less? The coinage of heaven is people. We can help populate heaven for Him if we do not flinch and draw back from the testing, proving, and refining that faces His chosen ones. The furnace of affliction is bearable when He is in it with you.

CHAPTER 21

An Unfinished Story

On Monday, December 5, 1978, I spoke for a CWC luncheon at the exclusive Roof Top Restaurant on Bonita Beach, in Bonita Springs, Florida. The place was filled to overflowing. Earlier in the year I had been on a national Christian television program, which had just been released to the Naples and Bonita Springs areas. The women, it seemed, were eager to meet the person they had seen on TV.

There were many decisions for Christ that day, but one in particular I shall never forget. I found myself addressing one woman especially as I talked. Later, as the ladies were leaving and giving me their name-tags and making commitments to Christ, I kept my eye on the little waitress standing in the back who had been listening and watching. There was a pause in the line and she came over. "Pardon me, I don't have a name-tag, but I want you to know what has happened in my life."

"You have asked Christ into your life, haven't you?" I asked, as I took Barbara in my arms.

"Yes," she managed between sobs, "but there is so much I want to discuss with you."

I introduced her to the club chairman and other board members. "Meet our new sister in Christ." They embraced her warmly. She asked us to pray for her husband. The story she revealed is one that moved all of us.

Barbara and her husband, Terry, were teenage sweethearts. Her father discouraged marriage until they had matured. He suggested Terry join the Navy. She described the horrible scars her husband had, due to a near-fatal wound received while working under a plane.

He had joined the Navy, and they had not married. One day, while working under a plane and wearing the customary earphones which block outside noises, Terry did not hear the plane's motors revving up. He noticed the whirring propellers too late. The propeller caught him and sheared the left side of his face. He actually saw his left eyeball roll down the runway. The left lobe of his brain was sliced away.

That happened seventeen years ago, and it was a miracle Terry wasn't killed outright. During the first year he had 133 operations. During the following years he continued to suffer a succession of painful operations, to the point where he developed immunity to practically all drugs. He and Barbara later married and had five beautiful children. She has always worked to help support the family. In Terry's frustration at looking like what he calls "a monster," he became a recluse, staying home, cooking and caring for the children. In order to obtain even ten minutes' respite from the gnawing pain, Terry turned to alcohol.

All of this Barbara shared with us. Our hearts ached for this lovely girl. It was no wonder she asked for prayer for Terry. We gave her our telephone number and told her we were available. We then called Minnesota and had Terry's name added to our prayer chain. On our way home, Roald and I prayed for Terry.

At ten minutes to five the next morning the phone rang. It was Barbara. Bonita Springs was thirty miles from Sanibel Island. "Please, please pray right now. You said you would help anytime. I am calling from a phone booth. My husband is in jail. . . ."

That afternoon, while Barbara was making her commitment to Christ, Terry drank two fifths of liquor and while drunk got in his car, taking his nine-year-old son along. They drove two blocks, and Terry's car sideswiped a row of mailboxes and ended up wrapped around a tree. Terry managed to drive the car back to their home and left it in the driveway. He staggered into the house and began preparing supper for the children. About this time the police came and escorted him to jail.

Barbara's daughter called her mother at work and told her what had happened. By reason, it would seem the enemy was in control and had immediately retaliated for Barbara's earlier con-

frontation with Christ. But we know God can turn
bad into good for those who love Him. Sometimes
He has to take drastic measures to get our attention. Barbara and Terry were yet to learn this.

Barbara later confided that despite this calam-
ity, for the first time she felt perfect peace. When
she arrived home, she gathered her children
around her and told them about discovering the
reality of Jesus. Together, this mother and her
five children joined hands and prayed to the Lord,
giving Him their problems and asking Him to help
them.

Barbara couldn't sleep that night. "All night it
was as if a voice kept telling me to call that woman
[me] who had said she would be glad to help in any
way." This is what she confided in us later. They
didn't have a phone—the nearest one was a mile
away. Finally, early in the morning, unable to rest
and unable to silence the still small inner voice,
Barbara and a daughter walked to a phone booth
on the highway.

Here God performed another amazing miracle.
After Barbara had completed her phone call to me,
a woman drove up and told Barbara the phone was
out of order. Barbara answered, "I've just used it;
it's working."

"No," the woman insisted, "see, I'll show you."
Whereupon she inserted a coin and tried to make a
call—and the phone *wouldn't* work.

Barbara's final words to me had been that she
was on her way (walking) to the sheriff's office.

After she reached there, she promised to call and give us more information.

At that point I woke Roald and told him about Barbara's call. "There's a men's prayer breakfast and Bible study this morning. I'll share this and we'll all pray. Maybe we can find a way to help," he stated.

Shortly thereafter I received another call from Barbara. "Mrs. Stanchfield, is there any way you and your husband can drive me to the Lee County jail in Fort Myers? I'd like to see my husband and try to talk to the judge before his arraignment this morning."

Roald and I were really beat. The marathon of speaking engagements, the long weary miles of travel, and the virus that had sapped our strength considerably were all taking their toll. It would have been easy to tell Barbara, "Honey, we feel sorry for you, and we'll do the best we can, and we are praying. Keep your chin up. . . ." But we wouldn't do that. We know the Lord in His providence uses people to accomplish His perfect will. The Bible says ". . . faith without works is dead . . ." (James 2:26). This did not enter our thinking. It was not why we got out of bed, dressed, and drove to the aid of this new babe in Christ. But this is what the Word teaches. We are to be available to those who need help. We minister in Christ's lovely name.

On the phone I assured Barbara we'd be on our way. Then I asked her to join me in prayer. "God, we believe You are going to do a work in Terry's life through this latest experience. We claim him for You. We want this to be the beginning of his coming into a relationship with You. . . ."

In the cool gray of the predawn we drove thirty-five miles and picked up Barbara and her small daughter. Then we drove to Fort Myers and the Lee County Jail.

It was like something out of an old-time movie. Waiting in the reception room of a county jail was a new experience for us. We passed through a large front door into a room about twenty feet square, with a hardwood floor, dim lighting, and apparently no air conditioning. It was stiflingly hot, even at that early morning hour. The police matron was powerfully built. She loomed large and foreboding, a cigarette dangling from the corner of her mouth.

The desolate room boasted three hardwood, kitchen-like, straight-back chairs. People passed in and out the doors, performing their chores in a cool, perfunctory manner. There are a lot of places you would rather be. The Bible says when you are ministering to people in jail, you are ministering to Him. The idea of Jesus in jail seemed awful at that moment.

Barbara approached the police matron. "My husband was brought in for leaving the scene of an accident and driving with a suspended license while intoxicated. Please, may I see him?"

The answer was an immediate no. We learned

that in another hour the judge would arrive. We might stand a chance with him. We walked down the street and found a restaurant where we could have breakfast.

When we returned Barb and I took the two remaining chairs. An attractive young woman sat nearby, wringing a handkerchief in her hands.

Time droned slowly away, with all kinds of people coming and going. It was a great study of mankind in action. There was cold, unfeeling efficiency, with no love in evidence.

We struck up a conversation with the young woman. Her name was Joy, but she was anything but joyful. She and her husband had come to the area to look for work. They were staying at a reasonably priced motel. No sooner had he found employment than their car was involved in a hit-and-run accident. They could not collect on insurance. They had to get the car repaired in order for him to keep his new job. At the same time the motel bill was getting higher. They used what little cash they had to get the car fixed. Then the motel manager put her husband in jail for failure to pay a balance of $76 on their bill. It seemed their "luck" had run out.

Finally the judge arrived. Quickly Barb and I jumped to our feet and approached him. I introduced myself. "I've been in town as a speaker for Christian Women's Club. This young woman heard me speak, and her life has been changed. She called us this morning to tell what happened to her husband. At this moment Mr. Al Hartley is conducting a Bible study on Sanibel Island. He and men like Dick Brodeur (a prominent attorney on the island) are praying for Terry. These are dedicated men—we are all people who are willing to help people like Terry and Barbara Moser. I would like an opportunity to speak to Terry."

The judge recognized Al Hartley and Dick Brodeur's names. Within moments he had agreed to let Terry out on probation into our custody. Then Joy approached the judge and asked about her husband. He said he had done all he could in reducing the bail to $106.05. "But Judge, I don't have any money," she pleaded. He told her to get a bail bondsman. Joy, with tears filling her eyes, quietly left the jail. She stood outside sobbing, a pathetic and forlorn figure.

Just then Terry came out of the jail. We had steeled ourselves because of his appearance, but we saw an alive and handsome young man. Yes, half his face was disfigured, but we saw the real Terry. To meet him was to love him immediately. I hugged him, and Barb introduced us. "Terry, it's going to be okay. . . ."

Terry was responsive. But he had something else on his mind. "There's a fellow in jail who hasn't done anything, except he owes a little on a motel bill."

"Yes, that's his wife standing there," Barb replied. "We've got to help those kids," Barb said. "How much money have you got, Terry?" With that he reached into his pocket and took out his billfold. "Look, I've got a hundred," he said, and handed it to Barb.

Roald had fifty dollars on him, and I had ten. Quickly we ran to Joy with the money. She was overwhelmed. Moments later her husband walked out of the jail a free man. They were both overwhelmed.

Terry Moser has a heart as big as the out-of-doors. Barbara had spoken the truth when she told us what a good man he was, and how much he loved helping people. Terry immediately offered his home and help to Joy and her husband. We filled Joy's husband's car with gas, and they followed us back to Bonita Springs to the Moser home. There were four wonderful little children waiting for their mother and daddy.

On the return trip we talked to Terry. "God has arranged all of this, Terry. He is in charge, and He is the answer to your problems and to your life. Your wife has received Christ, and this is why God had my husband and myself here to help you. There are prayers going up for you all over the country. You are going to praise God this happened. This is really a miracle. . . ." Terry's parole was lifted, and the charges against him were dropped. Today he is a transformed man!

We gave Terry a copy of my testimony tape. "Promise me you will listen to it," I said. He promised. He not only did, but he sat his children down and had them listen. Then he explained to them what it means to invite Jesus into your heart. Later he went all over the neighborhood with the tape. When we left the family they were all LIVING FOR JESUS! Today, Terry the recluse joins his family at Sunday church services. He has been reborn and is free at last.

Later we talked to Joy and her husband. "We will never be the same" was their response to all that had happened.

When we got back to the island that day, we called Al Hartley (the cartoonist). He was overjoyed at how God had answered our prayers. Later that night he rang our doorbell. He handed us $150 and a gift of $5 each for the five Moser children. "This is a love gift with no strings attached," he explained. The men at the Bible study and prayer breakfast had wanted to share.

Christianity is getting outside of yourself and sharing Christ. This is just one of the many thrilling things that have happened in our lives as we have yielded ourselves to the Lord and tried to do His bidding.

But the story doesn't end there.

On December 7, 1978, I spoke at the exclusive Naples Beach Club. Barbara accompanied me, along with her girl friend and the girl's mother. There were many decisions for Christ that day, and among them were Barbara's guests.

It is so wonderful to be a part of God's ministry.

CHAPTER 22

Perfect Peace

When I was in my late forties it was discovered I had a huge, cystic tumor. I was rushed into surgery. I had been told the night before it might be malignant. There is always that possibility.

That night, in the hospital room, I received a telephone call from a woman I scarcely knew. "The Lord told me to call you," she related. "I want to give you a verse from the Bible. I know what you are going through right now, because I've been there. Wilma, I've had a hysterectomy, a mastectomy, and heart surgery. Isaiah 26, verse 3 has always given me perfect peace. 'Thou wilt keep him in perfect peace, whose mind is stayed on thee: because he trusteth in thee.' "

I opened my Bible, and the verse was already underlined. I thanked her and thought, *Well, isn't that nice of her.* I had been a Christian five years, but I still had a lot of growing to do. I lacked maturity as to how God works. The woman had explained that God gave her such peace and joy through that verse, that each time she'd been in the hospital she was able to leave a witness for

Christ, and people had come to know Him because
of this. "He has worked miracles before, Wilma,
for some of us. And He can do the same for you. I
am claiming that verse and that peace for you."

As I thought about that verse and what this
surgery might reveal, I suddenly felt a terrible
need for peace. I reached for my Bible and decided
I'd better read the verse again. Suddenly it minis-
tered to me. I would gladly go through that night
again to experience what happened to me. In a
sense I did enter the "valley of the shadow of
death" once more, but this time in my mind He
was with me every single step. I experienced
peace and joy and total release from fear.

*What if something does happen to me, Lord,
how would this affect Roald and Lisa and the
others?* I knew I would immediately be in the
presence of the Lord if I were to die, and this was
God's will. I knew this was the greatest thing that
could possibly happen, and I was overwhelmed
with assurance. But Roald . . . what about his
reaction?

Roald's mother had died of cancer shortly before we met. He was bitter about it at the time and
angry with God. I wondered how he would take
my death if it were to happen. Would he turn his
back on God?

I fell asleep praying, *Oh God, don't let that
happen to Roald.* In the middle of the night I
awoke and wrote a letter to him and to Lisa. "I am
in the will of God. I have never experienced such
peace and utter tranquility of spirit as I am expe-

riencing now. I am actually excited. Never doubt even for one moment that this is not God's perfect will." I wanted Roald to have that letter in case the surgery did not turn out the way he expected it to.

In the morning when they came to get me I was still wide awake. The letters were sealed, to be given to Roald and Lisa if something happened. When they got me to the operating room I found myself praying for others who were to have surgery that day. There was no fear. I kidded and teased the doctor in the operating room. Then that was it—zap! I was out.

In the recovery roon following the surgery, the nurse's aide who stayed with me said, "Can you tell me how you could go into surgery like that?"

"I have Christ in my heart," I told her. "The Bible says, 'Thou wilt keep him in perfect peace, whose mind is stayed on thee: because he trusteth in thee.' I kept my mind on Jesus." I shared with her and gave her a little Christian Women's Club book I'd brought along.

Later, when my doctor came around, he explained he had removed a tumor the size of a football. "But you had a fantastic surgery," he explained, "and it wasn't malignant."

Still later, after a few days, he came around again. "You are responding so well," he said. I kept praying, asking the Lord for the right opportunity to speak to the doctor. I knew he'd had open-heart surgery the year before.

One day, after the stitches were removed, my

doctor took a chair, turned it around, and straddled it. "Okay, what is your secret?" He surprised me with the suddenness of his question.

"What do you mean?" I questioned.

"You are real, real happy. I have not seen many people go into surgery the way you did. You had no fear, did you?"

"No, I had none," I answered.

He looked at a painting of Jesus my daughter had brought. "Did it have anything to do with that?" he motioned toward the picture.

"Yes, I know Him."

"How do you know that's the way He looks?"

"I don't know. That's just an artist's rendering."

"How do you know it's a Him?"

"Oh come on, doctor, the Bible says Jesus is God's Son. Frankly, I had a very close brush with death one time, and I was dying and I was being separated from God. I spent ten years with a fear of dying without God before I met that Christ. I met Him when He was simply introduced to me the way I am introducing you to Him now. Do you know He loved us and died on the cross for us, and was resurrected and is living today in heaven? All we have to do is appropriate the gift of Himself. And it is a gift. The Bible clearly says that to as many as receive Him, He gives the right, the ability, and the authority to become one of His children. I prayed and invited Christ into my heart, and He came in.

"Let me tell you about a Bible verse a lady gave

to me the night before my surgery . . .," and I gave him the Isaiah 26:3 verse.

He looked at me solemnly. After a while he said, "You speak or something, don't you? What is that organization?"

"It's Christian Women's Club. As soon as I get well, I want your wife to go with me. I found the Lord at one of their luncheons. They meet at country clubs and lovely places."

Then he remarked, "Do you know I had open heart surgery a year ago?"

When I told him I knew, he said, "They came in and gave me last rites, and I suddenly had a feeling of peace, too."

"That was Jesus, that was Jesus!" I said to him excitedly. "He was trying to communicate with you. . . ."

"I see, I see. That is very interesting. Okay young lady, I want to tell you your recovery is remarkable. You are healing faster than anyone I have ever seen. I do not need to see you any more. I am leaving for Washington. When I return I'll see you in my office. Call for an appointment."

When I went in to see him later, he was very business-like. But to my stepdaughter, Saza, who was pregnant and also seeing him, he said, "Tell me about your stepmother. What is that organization she speaks for? What does she talk about?"

Saza told him I talked about Jesus and said I had come to know Him as Lord and Savior. He asked her, "And you too?" And she answered, "Yes."

Saza saw him three more times. One night the Lord awakened her and told her to write her testimony. She did, and wrote a personal letter to the doctor in the middle of the night. She explained how years before she had seen a change in my life. She shared that at first she was resentful of what had happened to me, but then explained how she, too, met Jesus. She ended the letter by writing, "'Doctor, I love you in the Lord, and Wilma loves you too. This has happened in our whole family. Jesus wants me to tell you all this so you can really come to know Him, too."

The doctor received the letter, and within the week he was gone. A massive heart attack took him. But we had the assurance that God got Saza up in the middle of the night to write him as she did. We have no proof he invited Christ into his heart, but we feel in our hearts today he is with Jesus.

It all began the night before surgery, when one of God's faithful servants followed the leading of the Holy Spirit and phoned me in the hospital. Her call and that verse from Isaiah put peace—God's perfect peace—and joy into my heart. Others saw and wondered. What God did for me, He will do for anyone who looks to Him and trusts in what He has provided for our salvation.

CHAPTER 23

The Other Side of Death

When I appeared on a Christian TV talk show the host asked, "Did both you and your husband have an identical experience of going away from God when you were struck by lightning?" We did, with one exception. Roald really felt, as he saw the beauty of what I can't describe, that he was going away from the light. He thought, *Where is He? Where is God?*

I thought God would be there also, but there was no one. Both of us had the feeling that the light was going away, and when it was almost like a pinpoint, the glory receding, that then it was going to be over for us forever. For Roald the pinpoint was still there, but he did not know where he was. It was like looking around and asking "Where am I?" With me there was a sure knowledge God was not there. I thought, *Too late, too late. I am alone.*

We were still trying to stay in the game for the next ten years, and, as I have explained, it became like a ballgame in my mind. I would think, *Now I have another chance to run for home*—the ultimate destination where I would spend all eternity. I did not like articulating words like "heavenly home," but that was my goal. I was trying very hard to run, standing on third base, poised to go. When I finally heard the truth about Christ, it was like something inside me said, *This is it, Wilma, now's your chance to run.* When I made my decision that day it was not a blind leap of faith. I knew just enough to realize that what was being said at that CWC luncheon was truth, and this was my running opportunity. I am still running. When the day comes that I do die, I will have reached home safely.

Becoming a Christian for many is thought of as, "Well, I have got it made. I am on my way to heaven; don't bother me any more." It is like fire insurance. That was not the way it was for me, however. It became a tremendous adventure of trusting in Him.

As I began this marvelous adventure of walking and running with Jesus, and as experiences began to come to us where we were given opportunities to launch out in faith, and I knew I was really in the boat with Jesus, my phone began to ring. I was given many opportunities to speak and share. As books began to deal more with the subject of after-life experiences and what are called "out of the body" experiences (OBE), people recalled my story and wanted my reaction to statements being made in the press and on TV. Did I believe what

Dr. Raymond Moody and Dr. Elisabeth Kubler-Ross had written?[1]

The response to their books in particular has been unprecedented throughout the country. They appear to have brought to the surface the long-submerged questions and feelings of thousands of people. No one wants to die, and when people do face that reality they want to be assured there is life after life. These books tell of the "hundreds" of patients who returned from the threshold of death to report on the other side. What they reported was indescribable peace, joy, bliss, and happiness.

It was reassuring to countless people who had lost loved ones to the Grim Reaper. Death was not after all going to be the end of relationships they had known in life. As Joe Bayly wrote in *Eternity* magazine (July 1977): "The news is that we Americans have conquered the age-old mystery and fear of death. We have dispelled the mists that confronted philosophers from the beginnings of human knowledge. We have discovered the secret that kings and commissars would have given everything to know. There is life after life. . . ."[2]

But Bayly asks the question many thinking Christians have asked: "On whose authority do we

---

[1]Raymond Moody, *Life After Life* (Covington, Ga.: Mockingbird, 1975). Elisabeth Kubler-Ross, *On Death and Dying* (New York: The Macmillan Co., 1969).
[2]Joseph Bayly "Death After Death," *Eternity* (July 1977), p. 48.

accept the reality of life after death?" He replies
with the answer I found myself stating. "The his-
toric Christian answer, the only Christian answer,
is 'On the authority of Jesus Christ, who died and
was raised from the dead by the miraculous inter-
vention of God, never to die again. On the authority of those who were with Him after His resurrection for forty days.'

"No authority in the field of medicine, psychol-
ogy, or psychic research (and the three seem in-
creasingly entwined around the continuing
Moody-Ross reports) can increase the only true
evidence, which is provided by the resurrection of
our Lord. Nor can it increase our faith, except at
the expense of the Object of that faith."[3]

Soothing as it may be to people to read and hear
that life after death is all peace and joy, this cannot
be reconciled with what the Bible teaches.

During the interview that day on the TV program, I quoted C. S. Lewis. "We should never ask
of anything 'Is it real?' for everything is real. The
proper question is, 'A real *what?*' " There is abundant evidence that spiritual counterfeits exist. I
am in agreement with the *Journal of the Spiritual
Counterfeits Project*, which states: "To the extent
that the Devil can establish conditions which anes-
thetize the mind against the piercing reality of
death as curse and judgment, he effectively seals
people off from God and the gospel of Christ."[4]

[3]*Ibid.*
[4]*Ibid.*

That precisely is where it's at.

After reading *Life After Life* by Raymond Moody, I asked God: "Why was my experience so different from these I am reading about?" I went through a period of uncertainty. *What is wrong?* I kept thinking. Satan was really hitting me. I confessed this uncertainty to the Lord. "God," I said, "I give myself totally to You. My life belongs to You. Give me the wisdom to understand all this. Give me what I need to relate to those who are now questioning me."

My answer from the Lord was definite. *You know your experience, Wilma, recall it again.* I was headed into eternity with everything that had ever been wrong in my life—and it was a heavy load—and I was being separated from God. It was not at all glorious, and I did not feel the comforting presence of anyone. I was never so alone in my entire life as I was in that moment.

Not everyone's experience is the same, as documented by Moody, Ross, and others. But there are striking similarities—cessation of pain, a "Being of Light," no fear, anguish, or distress. People speak of feeling secure and loved. They tell of being met by relatives and friends who have already died. All is peace and beauty. The order of events and reported phenomena are similar, though not identical.

But there is a noticeable absence of references to anyone encountering anything like the biblical heaven. Jesus is not usually mentioned, and God is usually referred to as the "Being of Light." The few who do make such references speak of Him as having a sense of humor, being understanding, forgiving, and kind. The astonishing thing is that even when the panorama of their sinful deeds was made manifest before this "Being of Light," the "Being" responded not with anger and rage, "but rather only with understanding, and even with humor."[5]

That is not compatible with biblical teachings on the subject of sin and the consequences of not confessing Christ as Savior in this life. Jesus made the perfect atonement for sin while here on Earth, and unless we have acknowledged Him and accepted His offering, there is no salvation or access to His presence.

Zola Levitt and John Weldon, in their book *Is There Life After Death*, state they would have expected biblically oriented folk (who have supposedly had the OBE experience and been interviewed) to say " 'I saw just what I expected to see from my study of the Bible.' But no one has given such a testimony through the volumes of reported cases."[6]

This raises serious questions.

Levitt and Weldon tell it like it is. "We find that these life-after-death stories—particularly the good reputation of death as we are now coming to

[5]Moody, *Life After Life*, p. 70.
[6]Zola Levitt and John Weldon, *Is There Life After Death?* (Irvine, Ca.: Harvest House) 1977, p. 51.

see it—is something like positive public relations
for the entire occult movement. We suspect that
something much bigger than the innocent folks
who tell of these experiences and the doctors who
publicize them is behind all of this."[7]

If the Bible says one thing regarding life after
death, and the life-after-death people say another
thing, who is right? God, or science and research-
ers and writers?

Roald and I were returning from Florida, and I
had an important opportunity ahead of me to share
with a large church that had conducted a six-week
study on death and the books related to it. I had
been asked to attend the conclusion of the study,
because I was supposed to be a real, live OBE
exhibition that would pull their entire study together.

Actually, I was going to blow the whole thing
apart! Roald stopped for gas on this trip, and I
went into an adjacent shop and found a "Successful
Living" bookrack. I am always interested in these
racks and end up buying two or three books. I had
been praying and asking the Lord for guidance
and help in my preparation for my upcoming engagement. As I stood in front of this rack my eye
fell on the Levitt–Weldon book *Is There Life After
Death?* I knew God was in this and thanked Him
for this provision of help. (I heartily recommend
and endorse the book and urge readers to obtain a

[7]*Ibid.*, p. 56.

copy. Another good book on the subject is *Beyond Death's Door* by Dr. Maurice Rawlings. Dr. Rawlings describes Roald's and my being struck by lightning and our subsequent out-of-the-body experiences.)

As I read the book, I came to page 63, where the Lord spoke to me through a particular statement made by Martin Luther which the authors quoted. That statement convicted me in my heart, and the Holy Spirit clearly instructed me I had to go into that liberal church and unflinchingly declare the truth as I recognized it from the Bible. Martin Luther says:

> If I profess with the loudest voice and clearest exposition every portion of the truth of God except precisely that little point which the world and the devil are at the moment attacking, I am not confessing Christ, however boldly I may be professing Christ. Where the battle rages, there the loyalty of the soldier is proved, and to be steady on the battlefield besides is merely flight and disgrace if he flinches at that point.[8]

I thought of Anita Bryant, who did not flinch when the battle over homosexuality was being waged in Miami Beach. The world and the devil were attacking, and she recognized it. She professed Christ and the truth. I knew I had to stand strong for Christ.

Later, as I shared my story and convictions in that church, I emphasized that today I believe

[8]*Ibid.*, p. 63.

Christianity and God's Word are being attacked right here. The death and resurrection of Jesus Christ would have been absolutely needless if what we have been hearing about life after death is all true—that there really is no problem in dying, that there is nothing to worry about, regardless of how you have lived in this life, that God has a good sense of humor, and that our misdeeds will be shrugged off as if they never occurred.

Some now tell us life here is just a learning process to go through before we go on to the next life. It has always been the nature of the devil and his legions to counterfeit what God has established. The Bible tells us "Satan himself is transformed into an angel of light" (2 Cor. 11:14).

I told my listeners that to Dr. Raymond Moody's credit, he does say that the best way of distinguishing between God-directed and Satan-directed experiences is to see what the person involved does and says after his experience. Moody, however, says most of the people interviewed seem "loving and forgiving." But that still falls short of God's standard for entrance into heaven and life after death in His presence. The Bible clearly states (in many places): "For the wages of sin is death; but the gift of God is eternal life through Jesus Christ our Lord" (Rom. 6:23). Sin earns death; God gives eternal life only through Christ.

There is no way you can get away from the implications of Hebrews 9:27,28: ". . . it is appointed unto men once to die, but after this the judgment: So Christ was once offered to bear the sins of many. . . ."

The only way this life is a learning process for joy, peace, and a beautiful life in the hereafter is if you have received Jesus Christ. Until you have done that, it does not matter what you have learned or done here.

I thank God that as I fearlessly spoke that day in the church, there were those who saw the true Light. The apostle John explains it like this:

In him was life; and the life was the light of men. And the light shineth in darkness; and the darkness comprehended it not. There was a man sent from God, whose name was John. The same came for a witness, to bear witness of the Light, that all men through him might believe. He [John] was not that Light, but was sent to bear witness of that Light. That was the true Light, which lighteth every man that cometh into the world (John 1:4–9).

That is the kind of witness we are to bear to the world today. Light was originally found in a person—the person of Jesus. This was love operating, and the darkness of this world, with the vain imaginings of the minds and hearts of mankind, had eclipsed the way and the light.

One day it was as if God were asking me, *Why don't you start reading in Genesis again?* I opened my Bible to the first book. There I encountered the enemy at work. Satan in the form of a slithering serpent is in discussion with Eve.

And the woman said unto the serpent, We may eat of the fruit of the trees of the garden: But of the fruit of the tree which is in the midst of the garden, God hath said, Ye shall not eat of it, neither shall ye touch it, lest ye die. And the serpent said unto the woman, Ye shall not surely die (Gen. 3:2–4).

The devil is a liar and a scoffer. Initially he came at Eve with a subtle "Hath God said?" (v. 1).

As I read this, I saw this deceiver as an angel of light. His work of counterfeiting began with an innocent, unwary woman. God works in a natural way through our minds; the Holy Spirit calls to remembrance, and He recalled to my mind the apostle Paul's words "O death, where is thy sting? O grave, where is thy victory? The sting of death is sin . . ." (1 Cor. 15:55,56).

Quickly I remembered the words of Jesus:

And as Moses lifted up the serpent in the wilderness, even so must the Son of man be lifted up: That whosoever believeth in him should not perish, but have eternal life. For God so loved the world, that he gave his only begotten Son, that whosoever believeth in him should not perish, but have everlasting life (John 3:14–16).

The incident Jesus was referring to is recorded in Numbers 21. The people came to Moses confessing that they had sinned. The Lord had sent fiery serpents among the people, and when they bit the people, many of the people died (v. 6). They begged Moses to pray, "that he take away the serpents from us" (v. 7).

And the L ORD said unto Moses, Make thee a fiery
serpent, and set it upon a pole: and it shall come to pass,
that everyone that is bitten, when he looketh upon it,
shall live (v. 8).

Can you imagine anyone who had been bitten,
and who had been told what the Lord commanded
that they do, not wanting to look and live?

Jesus, in foretelling His death to His disciples,
said, "And I, if I be lifted up from the earth, will
draw all men unto me" (John 12:32).

I had often pondered why God would have used
the symbol of a serpent with Moses. I wondered
why Jesus said what He did about Moses and the
incident. Then it all fell into place. The serpent
symbolized the entrance of sin into the world.
That is what Christ really became. "For he hath
made him to be sin for us, who knew no sin; that we
might be made the righteousness of God in him" (2
Cor. 5:21).

Wherever I am asked to speak on the subject of
this new, "easy dying," I emphasize I am not
speaking against the persons who wrote the books
or their publishers, but that I stand in opposition
to the enemy of our soul who would dupe people
into believing they need not fear death. People are
being lulled into a false sense of complacency
which makes the Bible obsolete.

I ask people: Are you going to believe what God
says, or are you going to believe men and their
experiences? Read the Bible. Take the Word of

God and apply it to what you read and hear. The Word is your measuring stick for truth.

Truly, truly, I say to you, he who hears My word, and believes Him who sent Me, has eternal life, and does not come into judgment, but has passed out of death into life (John 5:24, NASB).

CHAPTER 24

In His Hands

I like to think of God as being a Master Artist who paints the canvas of our lives, if we will allow Him to do this. As He began to shape my life in my younger years through my father, who tried to guide me, I solemnly and suddenly decided to take the brush from the Master Artist and do the painting myself. I would paint me the way I thought I should be. As a result, the colors began to run, the objects of my life were out of perspective, and the marketplaces of the world found me without much value.

Then I reached a point in time when I willingly brought the painting of my life to Him. One washing of His blood cleared away all my mistakes, failures, and sinfulness. He cleared my life's painting and made it one that is becoming infinitely more valuable as I allow Him to continue His work in and through me.

Recently I read of a young girl who said to a seventy-five-year-old woman, "You are so beautiful." The woman replied, "Dear, I should be. I am seventy-five years old." In other words, over a period of time we should acquire a beauty that is apparent to the world, so when the world looks at us it sees the beauty of Jesus Christ, and less of us.

I think of God also as a potter. This came to me as I read a poem entitled "In The Potter's House."

When God wants to drill a woman
    and thrill a woman
    and skill a woman
When God wants to mold a woman
    To play the noblest part—
Watch His methods—watch His ways!
How He ruthlessly perfects
whom He royally elects;
How He hammers her and hurts her
And with mighty blows converts her
Into trial shapes of clay which only
    God can understand.
While her tortured heart is crying
And she lifts beseeching hands
    How He bends, but never breaks
When her good He undertakes—
When God wants to take a woman
    and shake a woman
    and wake a woman
When God wants to make a woman
    to do the Father's will—
    With what cunning He prepares her
    How He goads and never spares her
    How He whets and frets her,
    And in poverty begets her—
When God wants to make a woman
    and tame a woman
    and fame a woman

Struck by Lightning, Then by Love

He sets a challenge for her spirit—
Draws it higher when she's near it—
Makes the jungle, that she clear it—
Makes the desert, that she fear it,
And subdue it if she can—
So doth God make a woman;
Watch His purpose, watch His ways!
For God's plan is wondrous kind
Could we but understand His mind,
Fools are they who call Him blind.

Author Unknown

In 1977, after reading Psalm 77, God gave me a poem based on the familiar tune of a popular song. Because of verse 6 of that Psalm, I call this my "Song of Remembrance."

All of a sudden, my heart sings
When it remembers all these things,
How God loved me in such a way,
He sent His Son to earth one day,
To redeem my lost defeated life,
Filled to the brim with hate and strife,
And my heart healed with His gentle touch,
Oh Father God! I love You so much!

And Jesus, the way You take my hand,
To let me know You understand,
The way You cancel out my fears
Fill me with joy and banish tears,
You are my love, You are my light,
You change my "wrongness" with Your right,
When I remember all these things,
All of a sudden, my heart sings!

In His Hands

Holy Spirit, fill my soul each day,
And lead and guide me in "The Way,"
Reveal the beauty of His plan,
That takes me to the Promised Land,
Until I see Him face to face,
Pour out on me His mighty grace,
Comforter and Counselor be,
Open my eyes that I might see!

Dear Father, Son, and Holy Ghost,
Great "Three in One," You are my choice,
Most Triune God, You are my all,
You hold me fast, I cannot fall,
You—the Possessor of Heaven and earth,
Transformed my life, gave me new birth,
When I remember all these things,
All of a sudden, my heart sings!

I can have a singing heart, because I know I am
safe in the Potter's hands. Call Him a Master
Artist, Potter, Shepherd, whatever you will—but
call on Him. Before I was a Christian I found my
answers to the problems of life in the wrong
places. I was very fond of Omar Khayyám and
liked to quote his writings. Much of his writing
sounds romantic and poetic, yet it is despairing.
Many people see life this way.

Khayyám did say something that is right, however, when he wrote, "The Moving Finger writes;
and, having writ, Moves on: nor all your Piety nor
Wit Shall lure it back to cancel half a Line, Nor all
your Tears wash out a Word of it."

I memorized that. However, God says that

when we come to know Christ, He can wash away
everything and all can become new. It does not
take our piety or our wit, and certainly all our
tears cannot wash away a line of it. But God can.
The big difference is the word *but*. *But* changes
the picture. Our lives are not purposeless when
they are lived according to His plan.

   . . . but ye are washed,
      but ye are sanctified,
      but ye are justified in the name of the Lord Jesus,
and by the Spirit of our God (1 Cor. 6:11).